The *Norfolk Companion*

KEITH SKIPPER

*'Norfolk'
is not simply a word that
describes a county.
'Norfolk'
describes also a language,
a humour and a way of life.*
            Dick Bagnall-Oakeley.

© 1994 Keith Skipper
Published for Keith Skipper by
Jim Baldwin
Commercial and Private Publisher
Fakenham, Norfolk.

ISBN 0 948899 05 0

Typeset by Fakenham Photosetting Ltd.
Printed by Colour Print and bound by
Dickens Print Trade Finishers.

A Product of Fakenham.

Foreword

Colin Chinery, Eastern Daily Press

Amid the encroaching uniformity of English life, Norfolk stands unbowed, a beacon of rich authenticity.

Among its foremost light-keepers is Keith Skipper, whose inextinguishable humour overlays a serious love and understanding of his native county.

Norfolk, as the late Dick Bagnall-Oakeley pointed out, is more than a word to describe a county. It also stands for a language, a humour, a way of life. To which he might have added, an attitude to life itself.

The countryside of Norfolk, subtly changing across its undulations and wide-skied vistas, to Breck, Fen, Broad and coast, is one of the least spoilt in England. Geography has bequeathed an isolation that has shaped character and largely protected it. It is an experience which has given Norfolk a pronounced definition, and identity. The world beyond left it alone, and that was how Norfolk rather liked it.

The experience has given the people of Norfolk a self-awareness untouched by an irksome parochial nationalism found elsewhere. The true Norfolker has a self-confidence that is rarely strident and which comes in part from this sense of place. He is usually independent, hospitable, tenacious, and possessed of a sense of humour at once whimsical and pawky. If one were to select a word to describe the portrayal of native virtues, it would be 'understated.'

But in a levelling world that is losing its diversity of savour, these distinctive formulations have become increasingly exposed to the ascendent uniformity, which if essentially bland, is prosecuted with aggressive efficiency.

Norfolk cannot be insulated in a time warp, and the local need for jobs and housing ought to dissuade such quixotic notions. But realism is not synonymous with defeatism or indifference, or worse, a simple-minded belief that more means better.

In predatory calculations, Norfolk is seen as an underdeveloped market fit for exploitation, its distinctiveness and peculiarities without value, and rather a nuisance. Fields are to be built upon (though rarely for local people on low incomes), a cohesion breached, its voice diluted by the tidal force of a rootless lingua franca.

So Skipper is troubled by much of what he sees, and his unease is widely shared, Norfolk County Council's attempt to limit new housing development to a level appropriate to the county's true interest, has been overruled by Government, and a higher figure set. The unfaltering and destructive doctrine that Whitehall knows best runs counter to every Norfolk instinct and interest.

Yet there are those within the county who succumb to the Faustian promise, confusing change with invariable progress, and a proper urge to defend what is dear, with the metaphorical drawbridge of risible reaction. If you would see the workings of their theories (with acknowledgements to Wren) look around at the fate of counties from which many newcomers to Norfolk have been pleased to escape.

But Keith Skipper is concerned by more than population levels or housing design (as long ago as the early 'sixties, Correlli Barnett was inveigling against the 'Middlesex Look' then overtaking Norfolk villages).

Skipper is a protagonist for something less tangible, but what is the essence of Norfolk, that spirit of a people and a place which is the subject of this book. As English life becomes standardised – but paradoxically less homogeneous – Norfolk's distinctiveness sharpens in relief, and the need to value and defend it more urgent. In a county of Roundhead traditions, Cromwell's words take on a new meaning; a people that knows what it fights for, and loves what it knows.

In this book, Keith Skipper reminds us of our inheritance and what we are in danger of losing. It is a primer for newcomers, a refresher for the native, and a signal, that while Norfolk has always stood to 'dew diffrunt', we must do more than hope that Norfolk will be allowed to remain different.

Acknowledgements

This volume has been a fair while coming, although I am bound to say it arrives at a useful time in the prolonged battle to save Norfolk from turning into just another bit of the South-East concrete jumble.

Norfolk's glorious differences need to be constantly underlined and I am grateful to all who have gone out of their way to glory in those differences for well over a century. Apathy and ignorance may have dogged their missions but their resilience and inspiration make ideal companions while the same old enemies hound us still.

I am particularly indebted to John Kett for generous support in compiling my glossary of local words. I salute many others who have shown lasting affection for and a deep appreciation of our dialect. That illustrious list includes Robert Forby, Eric Fowler, John Nall, Jane Hales, Walter Rye and Arnold Wesker.

My large collection of local books, pamphlets and newspaper cuttings has proved invaluable in scaling a mountain range of facts about the county as well as in my sauntering across the plains in search of literary nuggets.

Colin Chinery, an old friend and colleague whose award-winning writing style illuminates the pages of the Eastern Daily Press, has provided a typically generous and stirring foreword.

Many other old friends helped me along the way after I had pounced upon their specialised knowledge and enthusiasm for the Norfolk cause. Just one more good reason for staying in one place a long time – you know where the brightest lamps burn!

Jim Baldwin again underlines his commitment to the local flag, and I thank him for his support in producing the book. Among those giving impressive pictorial backing – Clifford Temple, Brian Hedge, Alan Howard and Ron Shaw and his colleagues in Litcham Historical Society.

My final and most fragrant bouquet goes to my wife Diane for confirming her role as the best word-processor scholar in the Skipper household. She poured rich gravy over my Norfolk dumplings.

Keith Skipper
Cromer, 1994

DEWIN' DIFFRUNT

Dewin' Diffrunt

This book is about Norfolk's precious character and the need to preserve it.

Newcomers and visitors have parts to play, helping to break down a few barriers and to destroy a few myths.

I have been accused many times of being a fully paid-up member of the 'Drawbridge Brigade', of being less than generous in acceptance of change or the people who bring it. Well, I do plead guilty to defending the Norfolk faith at every opportunity, and I try to explain why in the following chapters.

They should add up to much more than a hymn of local praise. Hopefully, they will encourage those who have moved into the county, as well as the thousands of visitors who call each year, to learn a few of the verses or at least join in the chorus.

In this age of ready-made labels, the Norfolk native is stuck with several characteristics – suspicious, too deliberate in action and words, slow to bless and swift to chide, implacably opposed to any change. Legacies, no doubt, of being invaded and messed about many times over the centuries.

Most of those who have settled in Norfolk in recent times did not burst over the borders with rape and pillage in mind. (Big developers, all too often encouraged by distant Whitehall mandarins, have been regarded with darkest forebodings. In many cases, these forebodings have been fully justified.)

Most newcomers have brought with them an uncluttered gospel: we moved here because we like it and we don't want Norfolk turned into the sort of place we left behind. While we are flattered by the compliment, we can find a sting in this expansionist tale. If too many people move to Norfolk because they like it, chances are it WILL be relegated to the level of the grubby places left behind.

The same conundrum applies to the burgeoning tourism market, and constant cries about jobs and prosperity cannot hide stark long-term implications.

Home truths accepted and shared, we can get on with the business of highlighting qualities that give Norfolk its highly distinctive character. As the county attracts more residents, more holiday-makers, more interest, it is important to get certain matters right, or at least to give everyone a reasonable chance of coming to a useful conclusion. There are imponderables tied up with a cussed streak – when you qualify as a 'local' depends more on the folk among whom you are privileged to live rather than any fixed term of apprenticeship – but common ground can be found and tilled effectively if specific rules are heeded.

I'll deal with native demands first, simply because they are more important than anything else likely to surface in the campaign for peaceful co- existence:

* Newcomers must accept Norfolk people are different and praise them openly for it instead of criticising behind their backs.

* Newcomers and visitors should deliberately mispronounce Norfolk words and place-names to give the locals a clear psychological advantage.

* Jokes about passports, drawbridges, turkeys, ferrets, unhelpful signposts and close-knit families should be kept under wraps until a clear rapport has been established.

* Pub conversations should avoid most references to: housing estates, hypermarkets, dual carriageways, Estuary English, electrified commuters, and Ipswich Town F.C.

* All Norfolk schools should encourage the local vernacular rather than try to kill it off completely, and 'Squit' should become a GCSE subject before the end of the century.

* Newcomers and visitors must agree Norfolk people have a marvellous sense of humour, even if all evidence occasionally points to the contrary.

Observations of these simple regulations ought to make considerable inroads into doubtful areas where distrust and deception may have reigned too long. Now members of the indigenous population are asked to take note of the following guidelines:

* Norfolk natives must not gloat too openly or too often over their good fortune to be bred and born in The Promised Land.

* They should be proud to be different, but also capable of pulling up short of proving downright awkward in the face of banal questions or mystified looks.

* Automatic aversion to change must not be encouraged – except where it might have an obvious impact on what seems to have always been there.

* Jokes about furriners, estate agents, missionaries, Received Pronunciation, second-homers and outline planning applications should be kept under wraps until a clear rapport has been established.

* Pub conversations should avoid all references to 'them what move in an' try to tearke over'.

* Natives must accept that newcomers and visitors may never grasp the full glories of the dialect and its humour, but these should never be used to score cheap points – except in the village pantomime.

Friendly advice given and taken in the right spirit ... the only way forward as Norfolk squares up to more mighty challenges.

A few yarns to put you in the mood, or, if you are yet to be introduced to proper Norfolk ways, to act as aperitifs before the meal.

A Norfolk pensioner, asked for her views on the eve of decimalisation, said she thought it was a good idea. 'But I rekun they orter weart till orl the old people are dead!'.

A Norfolk mother sent a priceless note to the village school explaining why her lad was not present: *'Johnny ont be at skool terday cors he hent bin, but Iyre give him suffin' ter mearke him go, an' when heer bin, he'll cum'*.

Where else in the world could you expect such an erudite summary? And who dare suggest the meaning is not abundantly clear? The same goes for the powers of invention of the Norfolk labourer who did a hauling job, but was told he wouldn't get paid unless he put in a proper statement of account. After much deliberation, he wrote out the following bill:

*Three cums and three goes
at five bob a went = 15 bob*

He got paid in full.

THE DIALECT

The Dialect

For something supposed to have been on its last legs years ago, the Norfolk dialect is in remarkably good shape. It seems every time the funeral is organised the corpse sits up and mocks the pall bearers.

Even ardent supporters, including scholars like the Rev. Robert Forby, felt they were simply launching a final flourish in publishing their glossaries and other salutes to the local tongue.

Pointing to popular dialects in his introduction to 'The Vocabulary of East Anglia' compiled in the early years of the 19th century, Forby lamented: 'Will they not be overwhelmed and borne down by the general onset of the various plans and unwearied exertions for the education of all?'.

Harry Cozens-Hardy, who edited the first 'Broad Norfolk' booklet published in 1893 from letters sent to the Eastern Daily Press, prophesied the dialect would die out within a generation under the influence of the Board schools.

Well, a century later the local dialect has survived a considerable number of influences, including standard BBC English. All the last rites have proved premature, and chances are the preservation spirit will continue to make an impact deep into the 21st century. One of the reasons behind that survival could be the fact that newcomers will continue to be as interested as the natives in the peculiar dialect of the province in which they have settled.

It will take that sort of teamwork to fight the inevitable cries of 'Anachronism!'. The dialect will continue to suffer from dilution and it will have to adapt to stay afloat in some areas. But it is too strong, too precious to let go – and there's enough genuine affection and resilience among its supporters to defy any future campaigns to wipe it out.

The dialect has lasted best in more isolated areas, although some dialect speakers are 'bilingual'; they speak the local vernacular within their own communities but switch to Standard English for the benefit of outsiders or when away from their own homes. This sort of versatility will become more commonplace.

Indeed, it was evident over a century ago. Thomas Hardy captured the state of affairs well in 'Tess of the d'Urbervilles' (1891) when he wrote: 'Mrs Durbeyfield habitually spoke the dialect; her daughter, who had passed the Sixth Standard in the National School under a London-trained mistress, spoke two languages; the dialect at home, more or less, ordinary English abroad and to persons of quality.'

Many delightful words and expressions have disappeared with the trades and pursuits that inspired them. Horses ruled the furrows on Norfolk farms for much of the first part of this century. The old horsemen, and those who worked in associated trades like the blacksmith's shop, had a language all of their own.

My glossary includes some of those old words, out of sheer sentiment in some cases but also to underline a sad sense of loss. Stretching the memories of older residents is also part of the game.

As with all collections of this kind, some 'local' words may not be exclusive to this area. There are no firm rules for writing down dialect and so some items are open to argument. Perhaps that's half the fun of attempting to commit phonetics to print.

Our dialect originated from the speech of the Anglo-Saxon invaders, particularly the bands of Angles from the Low Countries. To their speech were added old Norse words from the Vikings who followed and a few later additions from the Normans and the Dutch.

At the outset of the 20th century many old country people had a vocabulary of fewer than a thousand words which had changed little since the Middle Ages. The mechanisation of farming resulted in a number of changes to Norfolk speech from the 1920s onwards. Of course, poets and other writers have saved many an ancient gem from extinction, and there remains a healthy output to satisfy an interest that varies from the simply curious to the downright fanatical. I include a list of recommended books at the end of the glossary and collections of useful Norfolk phrases and expressions.

Max Muller, writing in the Eastern Daily Press over a century ago, had worked out why people felt a deep desire to create in their local language: 'The real and natural life of language is in its dialects. Even in England the local patois have many forms which are more primitive than the language of Shakespeare, and the richness of their vocabulary surpasses on many points that of the classical writers of any period'.

The difficulties of writing in dialect are obvious, but love of Norfolk and Norfolk ways shines through all the literary ventures, be they in humorous vein or of a more serious nature.

International playwright Arnold Wesker set a trend few have seen fit to follow when he made genuine attempts to find out how Norfolk people talk for his play 'Roots', first staged in 1959. A few years working in the county, and marriage to a Norfolk mawther, clearly helped. He also took the trouble to include notes on pronunciation to help 'furriners' get somewhere near the accent and intonation:

When the 'won't' is used, the 'w' is left out. It sounds the same but the 'w' is lost. Double 'ee' is pronounced 'i' as in 'it' – so that 'been' becomes 'bin', 'seen' becomes 'sin' etc. 'Have' and 'had' become 'hev' and 'hed' as in 'head'. 'Ing' loses the 'g' so that it becomes 'in'. 'Bor' is a common handle and is a contraction of neighbour. Instead of the word 'of' they say 'on', e.g. 'I've hed enough on it' or 'What do you think on it?'. Their 'yes' is used all the time and sounds like 'year' with 'p' – 'yearp'.

'Blast' is also common usage and is pronounced 'blust', a short, sharp sound as in 'gust'. (I feel it is more of a 'blaarst'). The cockney 'ain't' becomes 'ent' – short and sharp. The 't' in 'that' and 'what' is left out to give 'thass' and 'whass' e.g. – 'whass matter then?'.

A useful crash course in the mysteries of the Norfolk dialect, but hardly put to good use by many companies presenting 'Roots' on television or on stages outside Norfolk. The same criticism applies to most other productions calling for a Norfolk accent – and complaints about the accent being so hard to imitate do nothing to take the sting out of regular disappointments.

To sum up, the best way to defend the dialect is to use it whenever possible. And if asked to give reasons why it should still be part of this high-tech, high-speed world, just smile and reply emphatically: 'Cors thass bloomin' bewtiful!'.

Glossary of Terms

Abroad	old Norfolk for outside: – 'Rough weather abroad, ole partner'	Arter	after – 'I reckon she's arter suffin'
Abser	an abscess	Athwast/athort/acrosst	across.
Accordinlie	accordingly – with emphasis on last syllable – 'accordinlie to him'	A'top of	upon – 'I saw Mr Jones a'top of his new hoss'
Ackulster	axle	Atwin	between
Addle	to thrive, usually applied to crops	Avels	awns of barley
		Ax	to ask. Past tense 'axed' – original Saxon
Afore	before – 'He dun that afore I got there'		
Afront	in front – 'Go yew on afront'	Babbing	fishing for eels, using as bait worms attached to worsted
Agin	against – 'I lent my bike agin the wall'. also again – 'I sharnt dew that agin'	Backstrike	to plough backstrike is to plough land already turned so that it is turned back again
Ahind	behind – 'I lent mine ahind it'		
Ahuh	awry, lopsided. also 'on the huh', 'on the sosh' (qv), 'on the slantendicular' (qv)	Backus	outhouse or scullery (back-house). Here the 'backus boy', the lowliest of servants, did most of his work
Allus/allust	always (pronounced ollus)	Badget	badger
		Badly	in ill health
Anend	on end – 'Raise that ladder anend'	Bait	food packed up and taken to work in the fields, mid-morning snack, elevenses, 'dockey' (qv)
Annic	to fool about, skywanicking (qv), nonnicking (qv)		
		Baldie-coot	a coot, from the white patch on the bird's head, just above the beak
Angry	painfully inflamed – 'My corns ent harf angry'		
Arsle	to move or wriggle backwards	Balk	ridge of land left unploughed

Bandy	one of several county names for the hare – from the curvature of the hind legs		a'rearnin, he ent a'cummin'
		Bents	coarse, rough grass
Bandy-wicket	old name for cricket	Bestow	store away or lay up for future use
Barley-bird	the nightingale	Betty/betsy	a kettle
Barleysel(e)	season of growing barley	Bezzle	to drink greedily
Barney	argument, quarrel	Bibble	of ducks, to search for food underwater
Barrow-pig	smallest on the litter also petman (qv) or pitman (qv)	Biddles	young chickens
		Biffins	variety of cooking apple
Bavins	light, loose faggots	Biggoty	overbearing, bossy
Bay-duck	shell-duck, from its bright colour like a bay horse	Billywix	an owl, usually applied to the tawny species
Beat	to mend fishing nets, hence 'beatster' a net-mender	Bishy-barney-bee	a ladybird. (Norfolk historian Walter Rye suggested it came from 'Bene Bee' – blessed bee. Ted Ellis, doyen of local naturalists, pointed out that ladybirds usually appear about St. Barnabas Day, June 23rd (old calendar)
Beaver	farm worker's afternoon snack		
Beck	a stream		
Becomes	best clothes, Sunday outfit		
Bee-bird	the great tit, so called because of its reputed partiality to bees	Blee	to reassemble, bear a likeness to – 'That mawther (qv) dew blee her Aunty Polly, that she dew'
Beetle	heavy wooden mallet		
Beezlins	cow's first milk after calving, a valuable ingredient in some old rural recipes	Black stalk	a chimney
		Blar	to cry, especially children
		Blood-ulf	a bullfinch
Beggary	large growth of weeds in a field of corn or root vegetables	Bolders	bullrushes
		Boke	bulk – 'There's more boke than corn in that crop'
Begone	decayed, worn out	Bolt	1. to swallow food without chewing – 'Dunt yew bolt yar grub ser
Bein'as	because of, on account of – 'Bein'as thass		

	quick'. 2. a bundle, particularly reeds used for thatching	Braze	to braze out is to insist one is right in an argument
Boodle/ buddle	the corn marigold	Brief	written or printed petition or begging paper
Bop	to curtsey, squat, duck one's head to avoid being seen	Brork/ brortch	to belch, to break wind
		Brotch/ broach	short stick, pointed at one end, a hazel rod used for thatching
Bor	local form of address for males and, occasionally, females too, although they are usually 'maw' or 'mawther' (qv). Some suggest it is an abbreviation of 'neighbour', but more likely it comes from Anglo-Saxon 'bur' or 'gebur', a householder or freeman, similar to the Dutch 'Boer'	Bronickle	bronchial. One of several mispronunciations
		Bruff	in good spirits, hearty
		Brumbles	brambles, general term for untidy undergrowth
		Buckhead	to cut off the top of overgrown hedge
		Bud	a calf beginning to show horns
Bosky	tipsy, merry	Buffle	muddle, confusion. (buffle headed)
Bottle-bump	the bittern. (or buttle)	Bulk	to throb – 'My sore thumb dunt harf bulk'
Bottle-nose	the porpoise		
Bottle-tom	the long-tailed tit	Bull's noon	midnight
Botty	fussy, self-important – 'She's a botty litle mawther'	Bumbaste	to beat severely
		Bumble-footed	clumsy
Bough-load	last load of harvested corn. It was customary to decorate it with leafy branches as it left the field	Bunny	bruise or swelling
		Bunt	to butt
		Burr	haze around the moon
		Buskins	leather leggings, gaiters
Braiding	net-making	Butt	a flounder
Brangle	to argue or dispute		
Brashy	land overgrown with rushes	Caddow/ cadder	a jackdaw
Brattlings	loppings from felled trees	Caffling	hesitating
Brawn/ braun	a boar	Caghanded	left-handed or clumsy

Cail	to throw weakly, wide of the mark	Claggy	sticky or lumpy
		Clammed	very hungry
Call	need or requirement – 'Yew hent no call to git upset'	Clamp	heap of potatoes or beet, covered with straw and earth to keep out frost
Canker	caterpillar	Clarty	daubed with syrup or juice
Carney	to wheedle, flatter, fawn upon	Clawth/clorth	severe pain – 'That tooth dew gi'me sum clawth!'
Carnser	causeway or raised road		
Carr	a clump of trees	Clever	special meaning in Norfolk of handsome or dexterous
Cat's ice	thin ice with air trapped beneath it		
Caution	remarkable event or surprising news – 'Well, if that ent a caution!'	Clinker	above average – 'Weer got sum rare clinkers ter year'
Cavings	refuse from threshing	Clip	slight blow or cuff – 'Clip o' the lug'
Cedar	a pencil	Clote	the coltsfoot
Chalder/scalder	a large number	Clunch	lump of chalk used in building
Chates	scraps of food	Clung	dried up or shrivelled, usually fruit or vegetables
Cheat	detachable shirt front, dicky		
Chelp	cheek, insolence	Coach	to stroke or fondle a cat or other pet
Chick	to germinate		
Chife	a small piece	Coarse	as opposed to fine as in 'a coarse morning'
Chimble	to slice or cut into small pieces		
		Cob	a seagull – and a horse (inland)
Chimbley	chimney also 'chimley'		
Chip up	to improve in health or circumstances	Cocky	a drain or small stream
		Coddy	stuck up, proud
Chitterlings	pig's entrails cleaned and fried	Colder	brick rubble
		Come-back	the guinea-fowl, from its call
Chovy	cockchafer or beetle		
Chummy	soft felt hat with a narrow brim	Cooms	ridges formed between horse tracks and wheel ruts
Clag	to clean or comb out matted hair		
		Cooshies/cushies	sweets

Cop	to throw a short distance		cut o'the skull!' 2. a picture
Cop-a-hold	to catch – 'Cop-a-hold o' that ball!'	Cuter/kewter	money
Coped	muzzled (referring to ferrets)	Dabster	expert in some particular field
Copper-jack	odd-job boy, main duty to look after the old copper boiler	Dag	dew or mist
		Daggly	damp, ragged
Coquilles	spiced buns eaten on Shrove Tuesday and Easter, particularly in the Norwich area	Damnified	indemnified – 'That ent no matter ter him, he's damnified'
		Daneswort	elderweed
Corf	cough	Dannies	a child's hands
Coughwort	the coltsfoot	Dannocks	1. hedging gloves. 2. small cakes of dough
Crimbling	to creep about sneakily		
Crome	muck-rake or implement with curved tines for clearing ditches or lifting root crops	Dans	year old lambs
		Dardle-dumdew	helpless or feckless person
		Datty	dirty
Crowd	to push along or drive forward – 'He dint harf crowd his ole byke up the hill!'	Dauby	sticky, muddy after rain
		Dawg/dorg	dog
		Deen	a faint sound, usually used in the negative sense – 'He never med a deen when he cum in'
Crow-keeping	bird scaring		
Cruckle	a crust (to grate or creak in Suffolk)		
		Deke/dike	ditch, or in some areas, a bank
Crud-barrer	wheelbarrow		
Cubelow	cupola, chimney of a malting	Develin	a swift, possibly from devil-bird because of its very dark plumage and swift flight
Cuckoo	cocoa – 'I hev a cup o'cuckoo afore I go ter bed'		
		Dew	1. social occasion or function – 'We hed a rare good dew down the pub'. 2. to thrive or succeed – 'His arly tearters dunt fare ter dew t'year'
Cup	command to a horse to go left when ploughing etc. (probably an abbreviation of 'come up')		
Custard	smack or blow		
Cut	1. a blow – 'I'll gi'yew a		

Dibles	difficulties, complications	Doss	1. to toss 2. hassock
Dickadilver	the periwinkle	Dow	wood pigeon
Dickey	a donkey	Drant	to drawl one's words
Diddleton Frank	a heron, from Didlington in West Norfolk and the call of the heron. (See also Harnser)	Draw	to clean out a dyke
		Draw along	move slowly
		Draw-latch	crafty or sneaky person
		Draw-water	the goldfinch
Didle	1. a ditching spade. 2. to dig or clean out	Drift	a lane
		Drug	vehicle for carrying felled trees
Didopper	the little grebe, probably from its quaint diving habits	Dudder	to shiver – 'all of a dudder'
Dindle/dingle	sowthistle	Dullar	loud noise – 'The boys dunt harf kick up a dullar'
Ding	slap or blow – 'Ding o'the lug'		
Dingin'	showery	Dumducker-dumer	mixture of various colours, so faded as to be indescribable
Dingle	opposite of make haste		
Dint	did not – 'I dint dew it'	Dunnock	hedge sparrow
Dipper	handled receptacle for dipping water from a butt etc	Durst/dast	to dare. (negative 'I dassent')
		Dutfin	bridle or halter for a horse
Disimprove	to weaken or deteriorate		
Dissables	underwear, from the French deshabille	Duzzy	stupid – 'Yew duzzy yung fewl!'
Dockey	labourer's dinner, taken to the field in a dockey bag	Dwany/dwainy	weak and sickly
		Dwile	a floorcloth
Doddle	a pollard tree	Dwinged	shrivelled (usually applied to fruit)
Dodman	a snail. (Also hodmadod, with variations in many parts of Britain)		
		Early-peep	twitch grass
Doke	dent or hole	Ecclester	axle tree of wagon or cart
Dop	short, quick curtsey	Eldern	elder tree
Dop-a-low(ly)	used to describe a short, squat person		

Elijahs/'lijahs	string tied round labourer's trousers just below the knee. Also known as Yorks or Yorkers	Fillister	carpenter's tool for cutting grooves or rebuting
		Finnicking	too particular, fussy
		Fintums	fuss over food
Enow	enough	Firplen	dustpan
Erriwiggle	earwig	Fisherate	to provide for, or perform a duty (probably from officiate)
Esh	ashtree		
Ewe	past tense of 'owe' – 'I ewe him ten quid'.		
		Fitten	feet
		Flag	a tuft of grass
		Flag-fire	bonfire
Faines	ghostly creatures once reported in the Hethersett area	Flair	to skin a rabbit
		Flapper	a young wild duck
		Flash	to cut a hedge
Fall	a veil	Flasher	a hedge-cutting tool
Fang	to seize hold of – 'She fanged hold o' me!'	Fleer	local pronunciation of 'flay' – to remove a skin or hide. Often heard in connection with cold weather – 'That ole east wind, thass enuff ter fleer yer!'
Fapes/thapes	gooseberries		
Fare	to feel or seem – 'He allus fare ter cum learte' – 'I dunt fare tew sharp terday'		
		Fleet	shallow, or a dyke or shallow pool
Farlans	shallow troughs used in the gutting of herring	Fleeten	to make shallow
		Fligger	fidget
Farrissee	fairy (also pharissee)	Floater	1. heavy fall of rain. 2. type of dumpling
Fathom	1. bundle of reeds for thatching. 2. to fill out or expand, referring to crops		
		Fog/fob	marsh grass
		Foison	juiciness of herbage – 'There's plenty of foison in the hay'
Faut	fault		
Felfit	fieldfare		
Fie/fey/feign	to fie out means to clean or scrape	Foisty	stale, mildewed. (Also fusty, feisty, fosey, ficety)
Fierce	1. fit, healthy. 2. inflamed, of a wound or skin infection	Fold-pritch	tool for making holes when putting up sheep enclosures
Filler/thiller	shaft horse in a team		

Foosey	*a withered vegetable, usually a turnip or radish*	Gaddy-wenting	*gossiping*
Foreigner/furriner	*anyone not a native of the vicinity!*	Gain	*handy, advantageous*
		Galleting	*driving flint flakes between flints when building, to prevent weathering and to improve the appearance*
Forgive	*to thaw*		
Fowlete	*crossroads*		
Fourses/farses	*afternoon snack in the harvest field*	Gallus-droply	*dirty or unhappy appearance*
Frail	*shallow basket made of rushes*	Galver	*to throb*
Frame	*to put on airs*	Gammarattle	*nonsense, rubbish*
Frank	*heron. (See Didlington Frank and Harnser)*	Gan	*gave, given*
Frawn	*frozen*	Gansey/garnsey	*jersey*
Frazzle	*to unravel wool etc*		
Frazzled	*frayed or worn*	Gant	*a fair in the village*
Frenchman	*French or red-legged partridge*	Gape-seed	*'He like his gape-seed' means he often stands and stares*
French mavis	*redwing*	Garp/gorp	*to gape or stare*
Fresher	*small frog*	Gastless	*stupid, thoughtless*
Frit	*frightened*	Gast	*barren, – 'A gast mare'*
Friz	*frozen*	Gather	*become inflamed*
Froise	*to fry. Also a pancake*	Gavel	*sheaf of carn before it is tied up, and a bundle of straw for the thatcher*
Frumple	*rumple*		
Fulfer	*missel-thrush*		
Full-flopper	*young bird ready to fly*	Gays	*illustrations, – 'He like ter look at the gays in the pearper'*
Funny	*remarkable – 'That rained funny hard last night'*		
		Get	*of a watch or clock, to gain*
Fumble-fisted	*clumsy*	Gimbling	*sniggering*
		Gladden	*wild iris or yellow flag*
Furrow-chuck	*whinchat*	Gloat/glat	*eel*
		Goat-sucker	*nightjar, from belief that these birds sucked milk from goats*

Golden drop	yellow plum	Haller/holler	to shout
Goldering	giggling, – 'Stop yar goldering, bor!'	Half-six/sixer	derogatory term applied to a pretentious person, may come from 'half past six', suggesting such an individual lay in bed for half an hour after the working man began his labours
Golpin/Gollerpin	swallow quickly, gulping it down, – 'He's golpin his grub'		
Good tidy	satisfactory, reasonable. (Or tidy good)		
Gorn	going, – 'I ent a'gorn ter dew it!'	Hank(up)	to fasten a gate or door
		Hap	to wrap
Goslings	willow catkins	Hapt(on)	met up with, come upon by chance. Also 'happened acrorst'
Gotch	jug or ewer		
Grane	to strangle or suffocate		
Greenulf	green finch	Hamper	to damage
Gret	great. – 'Thas a gret ole mountain'	Harnser	the heron
		Harriage	confusion. Probably from 'harry', to harass or lay waste. 'Gone to harriage' – gone to rack and ruin. Sometimes, erroneously, Harwich or Harridge
Greybird	English partridge		
Grip/gripple	small drain or water course		
Groundsels	foundations of a building		
Grundle	narrow, sunken trackway	Harry the Denchman	the carrion crow, from Harry the Danishman, better known as Harold Harefoot, son of King Canute
Grunny	a pig's snout		
Grup	shallow drain or rut		
Guler	yellowhammer		
Gushy	gusty, very windy	Haunt	a ghost
		Hayjack	whitethroat
Ha and hacker	to stutter	Haysel	haymaking season
		Haze	to put out in the sun to dry
Hack-slavering	talking in an excited way		
		Heater-piece	triangular piece of ground, such as a grass area at a road junction
Haddle	hurdle		
Hain	to raise, especially in respect of wages or prices		
		Hedge Betty	hedge sparrow. Also hedgeman
Hakes	hooks on which pots were hung by the fire, hence the expression 'black as the hakes'		
		Hen's noseful	a very small amount

Here and there	handy, or tidy and ship-shape
Herne	part of one parish projecting into another
Herring-spink	goldcrest
Het	heated. – 'Hev Mary het that kettle yit?'
Hid	head. – 'Mind yer hid, boy'
Higgle	to argue or bargain
Higgler	a dealer
High-larned	well-educated
Highlow	leather ankle boots for wet weather
Highsprite	ghost
High-strikers	hysterics
Hilda	elder
Himp	to limp. Himpy-lame
Hin	hen
Hinderpart	the back of anything
Hips	corners of a stack
Hissen/hisself	himself
Hitch(up)	to make room on a seat etc
Hive	basket trap for eels
Hobby	a pony
Hock	to kick or trip up
Hodmedod	snail (see dodman – more popular in Norfolk)
Hog line	'Brought up on a hog line' means badly brought-up, uncouth and ill mannered
Hold	to be in possession of money – 'Dew yew hold, bor, we'll go ter the pub'
Hold-ye	call of the boy (hold-ye boy) in charge of the horses drawing loads of corn sheaves in the harvest field – a warning to the man on top of the load. Also 'howdgee' 'howd' for the man in the load, 'gee' for horse to go on
Holl	ditch or dykes or a hole
Hollow-meat	poultry, rabbit – other than butcher's meat
Holy Boys	Royal Norfolk Regiment, probably originating from the Peninsular War, when the enemy thought that figures of Britannia (the regimental badge) were the Virgin Mary
Honky	temper
Horfling	moving clumsily
Horkey	social gathering and feast to celebrate end of harvest
Horkey-load	last load of harvest
Hornpie	lapwing
Hoss	1. horse. 2. to act boisterously, 'hossin' about'. 3. to hurry, 'Blarst, he cum hossin' along!'
Housen	houses
Hovers	floating masses of water-weeds
Howin'an-'mowin	chattering, gossiping

Howsomever	however	Imitate	to attempt, make an effort. – 'I shunt imitate ter dew that if I wuz yew'
Huckabuck	leapfrog		
Hucker	to complain or to stutter (see 'ha and hacka')	Iron-hards	purple loosestrife. Name comes from the tough roots of this attractive fenland flower, which were sometimes described as 'shovel benders' by men clearing dykes
Hudderin	large and unwieldy, usually applied to awkward youth		
Huddle	to pass the leg of a rabbit through the sinews of the other to enable it to be carried easily		
		Ivory	ivy
Huh	crooked or slanting, – 'On the huh'		
		Jacob	a frog
Hulk	to skin and gut a rabbit	Jag	term applied to a quantity of flints or other stones equal to about 15 cwt
Hull up	to be sick, vomit		
Hulver	holly		
Hummer	a lie		
Hunch	to push or shove	Jam	to plod or walk heavily, or stamp on
Hungry Ninth	another nickname for the Royal Norfolk Regiment, said to result from an occasion when the soldiers of the 9th Regt. of Foot sold their Bibles to buy food	Jannock	fair, honest
		Jatter	to shake or knock
		Jibbuck	to shake up and down
		Jiffling	fidgeting
		Jill-hooter	owl
Hutkin/ hudkin	a case or sheath for a sore finger	Jimmers	hinges made of leather, often used on sheds or rabbit hutches
Huxter/ huxterer	dealer		
		Jinks	five-stones or 'jacks' played by children
Ickeny	an adjective, emphasis on the first syllable, used in Norfolk to describe anyone who is aggrevating or difficult to deal with. Could it come from 'Iceni' who aggrevated the Romans in East Anglia?	Jip	aggravation, annoyance in the sense of pain – 'That give me sum jip'
		Job	anything remarkable – 'Her new hat wunt harf a job!'
		Jollificear-tions	fun, joviality

25

July razor	a scythe	Knap-kneed	knock-kneed
Jumpin' jacks	frogs	Know	information, knowledge, – 'Where dew he git all his know?'
Jurisdiction	management, – 'My man hev jurisdiction o'that'	Koished	thrashed
		Kyish	looking smug or shy
Kail	to throw	Laid	of corn, flattened by storms. Also ponds or broads frozen hard
Kedgy	agile, sprightly, used with reference to the elderly		
Keeler/killer	wooden tub used for scalding a pig after killing. Also applied to large tubs used for washing and brewing	Lam	to beat, – 'He dint harf lam inter him!'
		Lamper along	take big strides. Also lope
		Lanner	whiplash
Keppier-holt	instructions to a horse to go left	Larding	a beating
		Largesse	gift of money at harvest-time
Kelter	condition or state, – 'His farm's in good kelter'	Larn	(i.e. learn) to teach – 'That'll larn yer!'
Kiderer	pork butcher	Lash/lashy	watery or soft, often applied to egg with soft shell
Kinder	kind of		
Kinder-kinder	not in the best of health	Last o' the meddlers	a remark usually made to over-inquisitive children, meaning something like 'curiosity killed the cat'
King George	peacock butterfly. Also applied to red admiral and tortoiseshell		
King Harry	gold finch	Latch	to catch on or become entangled
Kiss-me-at-the- garden-gate	pansy	Latch-lifter	small sum of money, just enough to buty a drink, i.e. enter the door of the pub
Kit	a fish basket		
Kittywitches	cockchafer beetles. Also 'women of lowest order' who once begged in streets of Yarmouth wearing disguises	Leasty	damp, drizzly
		Lickup	small quantity, dollop, as if it were no more than the cat can lick up by one stroke of the tongue
Knap	to shape flints, – flint knapping		

Lig	to pull or drag along	Mash/mesh	marsh
Ligger	1. a plank bridge over a ditch. 2. short rod used in ridge thatching. 3. item of fishing tackle, usually used when pike or eel fishing	Master	expresses admiration. – 'Thass a master gret howse'
		Masterpiece	astonishing. – 'Well, I shunt never ha'believed it. Thass a masterpiece!'
Lijahs	straps round the trousers, just below the knees	Matchly	corresponding, well-fitting
		Matters	to feel 'no matters' means out-of-sorts, poorly
Lints	fishing nets	Mavis/mavish	song-thrush
Livelong	dandelion		
Lode	man-made water course	Maw/mor	local form of greeting for women-folk
Loke	lane or alley, usually enclosed		
		Mawkin	a scarecrow
Lollop	to progress slowly	Mawther	girl or young woman. – 'She's a nice young mawther'
Lond	small piece of land, part of a divided plot		
Long-dog	a greyhound	Mazy	1. sickly. 2. description of shotten or inferior herring
Lucom	a dormer window or barn slit		
Lumberin'	a noise	Meals	sand-dunes
Lummox	clumsy or ungainly person. – 'Git yew out o' the way, yew gret lummox!'	Meager/mearger	long handled reap hook for cutting weeds
		Meece/meezen	mice
Malted	hot and sweaty	Merrimills	sand hills
Mank	to toy with food. See also 'pingle'	Merrymay	mayfly or dragonfly
		Midder	meadow
March-birds	frogs (corruption of marsh-birds)	Middlin'	in fairly good health. – 'fair to middlin'
Mardle	1. to gossip, chat at leisure. 2. a village pond	Midnight woman	midwife
		Miller	moth
Mardlins	duckweed or ducklings	Million	pumpkin
Marrams	coastal sand dunes planted with marram grass to prevent erosion		

Mine	'She come to mine' instead of 'She came to my house'. Similarly with his, yours etc. 'He come up ours Saturday an' we go round his o'Sundays'	Morth	a moth
		Mouse-hunt	a stoat
		Mow in	join in
		Mucher	something of good quality. Usually used in the negative – 'That there ent a mucher'
Mingins	gnats, midges		
Minifer	stoat or weasel (cf ermine)	Muckup	a manure heap
		Muckwash	hot and bothered – 'all of a muckwash'
Minify	to make little of – opposite to magnify!		
		Muddled	referring to the moon, partly hidden by cloud
Misery	severe pain. – 'She suffer with a misery in har stummick'		
		Mud-scuppit	long handled scoop for cleaning out ditches
Mislen-bird	fieldfare	Muir-hearted	tender hearted or easily moved
Mislen-bush	mistletoe		
Mite	a little bit. – 'I dew fare a mite hungry'	Mumpers	carol singers or performers of traditional plays at Christmas. In Norwich beggars went mumping on St.Stephen's Day
Mitchama-dor	cockchafer beetle		
Mizzle	drizzle		
Mob	to scold, tell off. – 'She dint harf mob them kids'		
		Nailer	determined or domineering person
Mocking	placed or planted alternatively, in rows, especially trees in orchards		
		Nasty-particular	fastidious, precise
		Native	place of birth – 'He hent never left his native'
Moderate	in health, not too well		
Moise	to thrive, get better	Neat'us/nettus	cattle shed
Moll	a mole		
Monge	to eat greedily	Neck'un	neckerchief
Morfrey/morphrey	tumbril which could be converted into a wagon. (cf hermaphrodite)	Neesen	nest of birds
		Nest-gulp	smallest bird in the nest
		Nevvy	nephew
Mort	a large number (probably from Icelandic fishermen)	Nice	fussy, particular
		Nijerting	acting as midwife

Noah's arms	cumulus clouds	Paddock/puddock	toad
Nobby	a young colt	Page	boy assisting a shepherd
Noggin	brickwork between timbers in buildings	Paigle/pagle	cowslip
Nointer	rascal	Painted ladies	applied to kippers after they had been dyed before being smoked
Nonnicking	fooling about, horseplay		
Norweigan bishops	towering thunder clouds (beeskeps)	Pamment	paving stone or pavement
		Pample	1. to walk lightly on tiptoe. 2. to fidget
Nosings	white quadrants painted on bows of wherries		
Numb-chance	stupid. – 'Lookin' like numb-chance in a saw-pit' means looking lost or vacant when action is called for	Pan	to press down or crush. Heavy vehicles may be said to 'pan' agricultural land, making cultivation difficult
		Pangle	a badly-drained field
		Parish lantern	the moon
Nye	brood of pheasants		
		Par-yard	bullock yard
Oat flights	chaff from oats	Pass/passe	temper
Olive	oyster-catcher	Pattens	old Fenland name for skates, especially those with blades turned up in front
Ollands	old pastures ploughed up for crop growing		
One journey	working without stopping for meals	Pawking	beachcombing or collecting sticks for kindling
Oven-bird	bluetit or long-tailed tit, from shape of the nest		
		Paxwax	gristle in meat
Overgive	to thaw	Pearks	gadgets, inventions – 'I dunt hold wi'orl these modin pearks'
Overwart	athwart or across, with reference to harrowing land		
		Ped	a basket (cf pedlar)
Owler	old term for a smuggler of wool	Peerking	looking for something, nosing around
		Pensy	fretful
Packrag Day	old Michaelmas day – moving day for many on account of change of employment	Perk	to perch. Also a rather irreverent nickname for the top of the rood screen in church

Petman	*smallest pig in the litter*	Pod	*belly*
Petty	*outdoor lavatory. Possibly from the French 'petit' – small – the smallest room*	Poke-cart	*miller's cart for carrying 'pokes' or sacks*
		Polly dishwasher	*pied wagtail (also Nanny dishwasher)*
Pick-cheese	*bluetit*	Pollywiggle	*tadpole. Other versions include pot-ladle*
Pie-wipe	*lapwing*		
Pig	*1. a woodlouse. 2. tapering course of bricks laid to correct levels, occasionally seen in old buildings*	Popple	*1. poplar tree 2. nonsense*
		Potchet	*piece of broken pottery*
		Prating	*noise hens make after laying*
Pightle	*small field or enclosure*	Pricker bag	*farmworkers' dinner bag*
Pingle	*to toy with food (qv mank)*	Primmicky	*putting on airs, or finnicky*
Pinpaunches	*winkles*	Pritch	*1. to prick. 2. eel-gaff with three prongs*
Pipy	*descriptive of a plant run to seed, shot*	Proper	*undoubted, obvious*
Pishamire	*ant. There are several variations*	Prugging about	*wandering about*
Pishamire barney-bee	*earwig. (Combination of words for ant and ladybird.)*	Puckaterry	*muddle or confusion, distress (cf purgatory)*
		Pudding-poke	*long-tailed tit, from the shape of its nest*
Pitcher	*man loading sheaves of corn on to wagon*	Puet	*black-headed gull*
Pivet	*privet*	Pug	*wash a few clothes through quickly, – 'Just pug these through'*
Plancher	*a wooden floor*		
Plantin'	*plantation of young trees*	Puke	*disagreeable person*
Plate	*the tyring platform at a smithy on which the heated iron tyre was positioned round a wooden wheeol*	Pulk/pulk-hole	*small pond or spring of water*
		Pummace/ pommace	*pulp from apples used in cider-making*
Plawks	*hands*	Push	*a boil or carbuncle*
Plump	*bread soaked in hot water to which butter, sugar or dripping has been added*	Putter	*to nag, mutter to oneself. ('u' as in nut)*
		Putting on his parts	*misbehaving, trying to get his own way*

Pwidge	a puddle	Reasty	rancid
Quackle/ quaggle/ squackle	to choke or strangle – 'This here new collar wholly fare ter quackle me!'	Reed-pheasant	bearded tit
		Reel-a-bobbin	cotton reel
Quant	punt pole used on Broads or to use such a pole	Reemer	1. an expert. 2. a heavy rain
Queer	sick, out-of-sorts – 'I dunt harf feel queer'	Rhizzes	hazel branches, formerly used in wattle and daub building
Quick	twitch or couch-grass		
Rabbit	in carpentry, to rebate or cut grooves	Riffle	to break up the surface of a field by shallow cultivation
Rafty	with reference to weather, damp, chilly and windy	Rightside	to beat a naughty child
		Rigs	space between furrows on ploughed land
Rainbird	green woodpecker, its tapping considered a sign of rain	Rimer	a rime frost
		Ring-dow	ringdove or pigeon
Rally	shelf built into a wall	Ringes	lines or rows of trees or plants
Randan	second sifting of meal at the flour mill	Roaring boys	men who salted herring
Ranny	a shrew mouse	Roding	clearing dykes
Rare	often used in connection with anything unusual or remarkable, as an adjective or adverb. Sometimes rendered as 'rea' – abbreviation of 'real'. – 'Thass a rare ole muddle' and 'He travel rare fast'	Roger/ Roger's blast	a small whirlwind, usually regarded as a sign of unsettled weather
		Roke	mist or fog. (rokey or roky)
		Roment	1. rumour or tall story. 2. to spread a false report
		Ronds	marshy borders of a river
Rather of the ratherest	intoxicated	Room of/ rume o'	instead of, in place of – 'I see he hev got greenhouse room of his gardenshed what he took down'
Rattick/ rattock	noise		
Raw	annoyed, angry. – 'He wunt harf raw'	Rootling	burowing, rooting, usually connected with pigs
Razor-grinder	nightjar		

Rorping	*a loud noise as of a bull bellowing*	Sawney	*foolish, Usually used in confessing to doing something silly – 'Ent I an ole sawney!'*
Roughing	*turning in the heels of horse-shoes to form calkins, or small spurs, to prevent the horse slipping in icy weather*		
		Scald	*highest part of a field*
		Scalder	*a large number, a crowd*
Rows	*narrow streets of old Yarmouth, once numbering over a hundred*	Scissor-grinder	*grasshopper warbler*
		Scores	*path down cliffs, or narrow streets leading to beach*
Rub	*stone for sharpening tools*	Scorf	*to scoff*
Rubbidge	*rubbish or weeds*	Scrab/scrorp	*to scratch*
Ruck	*to crease*	Screws	*rheumatic pains*
Rum'un	*strange one – 'Thass a rum'um'. Also used to describe a bit of a lad – 'He ent harf a rum'um!'*	Scrouging	*crowding together, crushing*
		Scud	*to shake herring out of the nets*
Run	*to leak, with reference to kettles, watering cans etc*	Scuppit	*a scoop or ditching tool*
		Scutes	*projecting angles of an irregularly-shaped field, often presenting difficulty when ploughing*
Runnel	*a wheel*		
Runcie	*a cart horse*		
Sadly	*poorly, unwell*	Seal/sele	*a time or season*
Sail-reaper	*horse-drawn harvester, with which up to ten acres of corn could be cut in a day*	Seam	*lard or dripping. 'Bread and seam' once made many a meal*
		Sea-pie	*oyster catcher, from its pied plumage*
Sally/Sarah/Sukey	*a hare*	Seat	*sitting, of eggs*
Sammucking	*wandering, strolling aimlessly*	Sed-lip	*container suspended from shoulders in front of the body for use when broadcasting seed or fertiliser*
Santer	*a stroll*		
Sase	*layer of large flints occurring in chalk*	Seed-fiddle	*appliance for sowing, seed scattered from a*

	container by means of a wheel turned by the action of a bow with a leather thong	Shig/shug	*to shake or wave about*
		Shim	*the blaze on a horse's face*
		Shives	*small splinters of wood in the finger*
Seft	*saved*		
Seggs	*rushes (from sedge)*	Shock	*group of sheaves of corn in the harvest field*
Several/savrul	*a considerable number, usually more than the word suggests. A crowd of 20,000 at Carrow Road draws the Norfolk response – 'Savrul there!'*	Shod	*past tense of shed, with reference to taking off clothing. – 'He was that hot he shod his jacket'*
		Shoof	*a sheaf of corn*
Shack	*1. to wander around. 2. grain lying in the field after harvest. 3. to turn out animals or poultry on the harvested field to feed on any remaining grain*	Shot	*1. a young boar pig. 2. of plants run to seed*
		Shrog	*rough-coated or diseased rabbit or other animal*
		Shruck	*past tense of shriek – 'She shruck wi' larfter'*
Shack-time	*period in autumn for gleaning or 'shacking'*	Shruff	*twigs and sticks for making a fire*
Shammock	*a slovenly girl*	Shuck	*the shell of peas, or to shell anything*
Shannock	*native of Sheringham, and whose parents were both born in the town. Some insist grandparents as well*	Shucky/shuckety	*untidy, slovenly*
		Shud	*shed*
		Shufflewing	*hedge sparrow*
Shanny	*excited, wild, scatterbrained*	Shuft	*to move or push along. (to shift)*
Sharm	*to scream or shout*	Shug	*to shake or scatter*
Shat	*shirt*	Shutten Saturday	*day after Good Friday (Shut-in Saturday)*
Shay-brained	*silly*		
Sheers/shires	*counties outside East Anglia*	Shywan-nicking	*fooling around*
		Sibbits	*banns of marriage (or sibrits)*
Shell-carr	*variety of carrstone used in West Norfolk buildings*	Sight	*a lot, a good deal – 'I'm feelin' a sight better terday'*
Shet	*shut*		

Signify	to matter, usually heard in the negative – 'That dunt signify whether he come or not'	Smee	wild duck
		Smittick/smittock	very small piece
Sillybold	cheeky – 'Dunt yew be so sillybold!'	Smore	to throng or crowd
		Smoult	to become calm (of the sea)
Sisserera	a heavy blow	Smur	light rain or drizzle. Also used as a verb – 'That ent rainin' much, only smurrin''
Skep	big wicker basket		
Skinker	lad who fetched the beer at harvest time or filled the glasses and horns at ale-house parties		
		Snack	door latch
		Snaste	long wick on a burning candle
Skrowge	crowd together, squeeze, push	Snasty	bad-tempered
		Sneerfroys	supercilious
Skriggle	to squirm like an eel	Snew	snowed
Skunt	skinned, of knees	Snob	a shoemaker
Slad	flooded land	Sole	beat – 'He dint harf give him a soling'
Slade	a sledge		
Slantendicular	not quite perpendicular	Soler	anything surprisingly large in size – 'Thass a soler!'
Slarred	daubed		
Slarver	1. to dribble (saliva), drool. 2. to talk rubbish – 'He dew slarver on!'	Soller	a loft
		Sorft	silly – 'He's as sorft as they cum!'
Slop	1. a coarse drill material. 2. apron or working smock. 3. wet ground	Sosh	'on the sosh' means not upright
		Sow	a woodlouse
Slop-footed	walking with toes turned outwards	Spantry	threshold (also troshel)
		Spars	rafters
Slopping jacket	loose fitting jacket with large pockets	Spawle	1. to shout. 2. to spit out
		Spink	chaffinch
Slub	mud	Splar/splaar	to spread
Slummocking	ungainly, clumsy – 'A slummocking gret mawther'	Spolt/spoult	brittle, crisp
		Spong	narrow strip of low-lying marshy ground
Sluss	slush, mud, dirty water		
Smeath/smea	open area of low-lying land		

Spreed	to spread – 'Muck-speedin' time'	Stingy	unkind, harsh (pronounced stinjy)
Sprit	a quant or punt pole	Stive	dust. To 'kick up a stive' means to raise the dust, literally or figuratively
Sprung	split		
Spud	a weeding tool on a long handle or walking stick, also known as a dock-chisel or grubber	Stone house	a stone beer bottle
		Stoppages	epileptic fits
		Stover	winter food for livestock on the farm
Spuffle	to fuss or bustle about	Stram-macking	travelling around
Squat	'keep it squat' means to treat something as secret		
Squinder	to burn very faintly, like damp fuel which does not kindle into a flame	Strome	to walk quickly with long strides
		Strong-docked	well-built, thick-set about the hips and thighs
Squinny	lean and lanky		
Squit	nonsense, light-hearted conversation, an unlikely story – 'A load of ole squit!'	Strupe/stroop	throat
		Stulp	a post of any kind
		Sue	to discharge (boil or wound)
Stag	a cock turkey or a wren		
Staithe	landing stage	Sukey	a hare
Stam	to amaze or astonish	Summer lamb	the snipe (from its bleating call)
Stand up	to shelter or wait under cover		
		Summer snipe	sandpiper
Stank/stanch	a dam		
		Sunket	snack or morsel of food
Stannickle	a stickleback	Suslams	mixture of food, like trifle
Stark	stiff or tight	Swale	shade
Stew	cloud of dust	Swallacking	very hot (swale-lacking?)
Stewpe	to drink noisily, possibly from stoup – a drinking vessel	Sustificate	popular coruption of certificate
Stewkey Blues	cockles from Stiffkey	Swarston winder	a black eye. Could be connected with Swardeston or with Swart, meaning dark, i.e. a darkened window
Stifler	busy person, usually taking a lead. 'Hid stifler' – head man or leader. Foreman on a farm		

Sways	*hazel rods used in thatching*	Thillers	*gear for cart, harness*
Swede/ swedebasher	*native of Norfolk*	Thongy	*close or oppressive weather*
		Thredickle	*unsettled*
Swedge	*a blacksmith's hammer*	Tidiff	*bluetit*
Swidge	*a small puddle*	Tidy	*good or fair*
Swift	*a newt*	Tiller	*to throw out many stems from a root*
Swill	*basket containing 500 herring*	Time	*while – 'I could ha' dun that job time he wuz yappin' bowt it'*
Swimmers	*Norfolk dumplings*		
Swoddy	*soldier.*		
		Tipe	*pit dug for trapping rabbits – an old Fenland word*
Tack	*scythe handle*		
Tannup	*pocket watch on a chain (turnip)*	T'is an' t'aint	*sow thistle it is a thistle – and it isn't a thistle!*
Teamer	*a teamer or team of horses consisted of five animals, two to work all morning, two all afternoon and one resting, resulting in one day off in five. Teaman – man in charge of horses*	Titchy	*irritable, touchy*
		Tit-faggots	*bundle of small sticks used for fuel*
		Tit-lark	*meadow pipit*
		Titter-matorter	*see–saw*
		Tittle-me-fancy	*pansy*
Tempest	*a thunderstorm, rather than a storm of rain and strong wind as defined in the dictionary*	Titty-totty	*very small*
		Tizzick	*troublesome cough*
		Tom-breezer	*dragon fly*
Ter	*the, that, this. – 'Ter field look good ter year'*	Trave	*wooden frame in which lively colts were held for shoeing*
Tetter/ twiddle	*pimple*	Trav'us	*(trave house) – yard or open space near the village smithy*
Tewk	*redshank*		
Thack	*1. to thrash or beat. 2. to thatch*	Tricolate	*to decorate or repair – 'I'm gorter tricolate my ole shud', also 'tittivate'*
Thapes	*gooseberries*		
Thew	*thawed. Thow – to thaw*		
Thick-knee	*Norfolk plover or stone curlew*	Trosh	*to thresh*

Troshel	threshold	Wennel	a weaned calf
Trow	trough	Weskut	waistcoat
Truck	rubbish	Wet-shed	with wet feet – as opposed to dry-shod
Tudded	(toaded) i.e. bewitched		
Tumbler	a tumbril	Wheatsel	time of wheat sowing
Twilting	a beating	Whelm	to empty bucket or other receptacle
Twizzle	to spin or twist		
		Wherry	distinctive Norfolk Broads sailing barge, with a single huge black sail
Unean	underneath		
Ungain	awkward, inconvenient, clumsy		
		Whifflers	attendants who cleared the way for Norwich Corporation processions on Guild Days
Upright	to live upright means to have sufficient income without having to work for a living		
		Whippletree	drawbar to which horses' traces were attached on a plough or harrow
Useter	used to – 'I useter go ter the pictures'		
		Wholly	very, completely, used for emphasis – 'That cake taste wholly good, bor!'
Vacajees	wartime evacuees. (Also wacajees)		
		Wibbled	untidily packed
		Wick	nerves – 'git on yer wick'

Note: many words beginning with V take a W start in Norfolk – warmint, wittles and willage among them. There are also examples of the letter being changed in the middle of a word i.e. aggravating becomes aggraweartin'

Waps/Wapsy	wasp	Widdles	1. pimples. 2. ducklings
		Will-Jill	woman of masculine appearance
Warmint	varmint or vermin, troublesome person – 'Come here yew young warmint, I'll sort yew out!'		
		Will-o-wix	owl (also Billy-wix)
		Windle	small skep without handles, made of fine and skinned willows
		Winnick	to whimper
Wash'us	wash house	Wire in	to wire in means to eat ravenously
Weesh/ weesht	command to horse to go to the right		
		Without	unless – 'He wunt go without she go anorl'
		Witery	weak
		Wittles	food (victuals)

Woodsprite	*woodpecker*	Yellums	*bundles of reed for thatching. Yelming is combing thatch*
Worrit	*to worry or annoy*		
Wry	*fault or mistake – 'There ent a wry in'em' is praise!*	Yelt	*a young sow*
		Yisty	*yesterday*
Wypers	*lapwings*	Yoke	*to harness horses*
		Yorks/yorkers	*strings tied round labourer's trousers (qv 'Lijahs)*
Yarm	*to eat greedily*		
Yarmandering	*talking at length, reminiscing*	Yourn	*yours*
		Yow	*to yell or chatter or howl (To fretful child during a meal – 'Evy time yew yow, yew lose a chow').*
Yarmouth capon	*a red herring*		
Yelk	*yolk of an egg*		

Old John saved up to buy a bike. He told his pals on the farm, 'Now I kin hoss over to Swaffham ter see my sister Sundays.' On the Monday morning they asked how he had got on. 'Well, by the time I git ter Dereham, I wuz proper wore owt, so I tanned rownd an' cum hoom again.'

'But thass only harf way' they said. 'I know' said John with a smile. 'I'll hatter dew the uther harf next week.'

Dialect Books

Books written about and in the Norfolk dialect remain popular, although several have long been out of print. Here's a list of recommended reading, including the poems of John Kett and Bible stories written in the Norfolk dialect by Colin Riches.

Broad Norfolk : being a series of articles and letters reprinted from the Eastern Daily Press. Published 1893 by Norfolk News Co., Norwich, editor H. T. Cozens-Hardy.

W. N. Dew : A Dyshe of Norfolk Dumplings. First published 1898, by Jarrold Publishers. Republished 1973.

Ida Fenn : Tales of a Countryman: stories of The Boy Jimma in Norfolk dialect. Published 1973 by Reeve, Wymondham.

Robert Forby : The Vocabulary of East Anglia. Two volumes originally published in 1830. Reprinted 1970 by Latimer Trend & Co. Ltd.

Eric Fowler (who wrote under the pseudonym of Jonathan Mardle): Broad Norfolk written by the Readers of the Eastern Daily Press, January 21st–March 19th, 1949. Published 1949. Broad Norfolk, published 1973 by Wensum Books, Norwich.

Edward Gillett : The Song of Solomon in the Norfolk Dialect. From the authorised English version. First printed 1861, published 1862 by Thew, King's Lynn. Republished 1993 by Larks Press, Guist Bottom, East Dereham.

Sidney Grapes : The Boy John Letters. First published in volume form by Norfolk News Co., 1958. Published by Wensum Books, 1974.

Lilias Rider Haggard : Edited I Walked By Night, being the Life and History of the King of the Norfolk Poachers. First published in 1935 by Nicholson and Watson, London. She also edited The Rabbit Skin Cap, a tale of a Norfolk countryman's youth. First published 1939. Reprinted by the Norfolk Library 1974, 1975, 1976.

John Kett : Three volumes of dialect poems – Tha's a Rum'un, Bor, 1973, Tha's a Rum'un Tew published 1973 by Baron Publishing, Woodbridge, and Watcher Bor published by Wensum Books, 1979.

Mary Mann : The Fields of Dulditch, first published 1902. Reissued 1976, Boydell Press, Ipswich. Tales of Victorian Norfolk, published by Morrow & Co., Bungay, 1991.

John Greaves Nall : Glossary of the Dialect and Provincialisms of East Anglia, originally published in 1866 by Longmans, Green, Reeder and Dyer, London.

Old Barney : Broadcasts on BBC Radio Norfolk in three volumes edited by Keith Skipper. Dew Yew Keep A'Troshin' 1984, Down at the Datty Duck, 1985, and Dunt Fergit Ter Hevver Larf, 1986. All published by Jim Baldwin, Fakenham.

Colin Riches : Bible stories in the Norfolk dialect, Dew Yew Lissen Hare, published 1975 by George Nobbs Publishing, Orl Bewtiful an' New published 1978 by F. Crowe & Sons Ltd, Norwich.

Walter Rye : Glossary of Words Used in East Anglia published 1895 for the English Dialect Society by Henry Frowde, Oxford University Press.

James Spillings : Sketches in a dialect in Eastern Counties stories in the language of the people, published 1880 by Jarrold & Sons Ltd., Norwich.

B. Knyvet Wilson : Norfolk Tales and Memories, published 1930 by Jarrold & Sons Ltd., Norwich. More Norfolk Tales and Memories, 1931, Jarrold & Sons Ltd.

Arnold Wesker : The Wesker Trilogy, including Roots, published 1984 by Penguin Books Ltd., Harmondsworth, Middlesex.

There are many dialect articles to be culled from old copies of both the Norfolk Magazine and the East Anglian Magazine. For many years Maurice Woods contributed Harbert's News from Dumpton to the Norwich Mercury series of weekly newspapers.

Some Useful Norfolk Phrases and Expressions

Afore yer mother bort a shovel – the matter referred to is clearly over the head of the person being addressed.

All the way ter Swoffum ter dew a day's troshin' fer noffin' – Norfolk people's favourite caricature of their own dialect, delivered in an exaggerated drawl.

Alonger me – often heard in the pub with: 'What are yew a'gorn ter hev alonger me?' The offer is not made too loudly.

Angular Tellerwishun – makes a change from the BBC!.

Arn't them winders dear! – Norfolk husband trying to persuade his wife to keep a tight hold on her purse – and his wallet.

Are yew gorter cum? – a neat trick to manage both at the same time.

Are yew orryte, ole bewty! – local inquiry that hardly requires an answer – just a smile.

Aylsham treat – basically designed for the self-sufficient or anti-social. It means to treat yourself, pay your own way.

Best part of sum tyme – taking a fair while.

Betterannerhebbin – opposite to 'wassanwotterwuz'.

Bit here and there – a handy sort of lad.

Bit slow in cummin' forrard – traditional Norfolk trait of being reluctant to seek the limelight.

Bred and born – Norfolk purists insist this is the proper order as they correct those who talk of being 'born and bred' in these parts.

Cor, blarst me! – a favourite expletive along 'Well, I'll be blowed!' lines and often used as a prelude to a greeting.

Cum on in out onnit – useful advice to someone standing in the rain.

Cum yew up ter mine – invitations to friends and relations.

Dark over Will's mother's – signs of bad weather coming. Will's mother is not confined to Norfolk.

Dew yew keep a'troshin! – keep at it, keep going. The Americans might say 'Keep on truckin'!'. Troshin' is a local corruption of threshing ... sorting out the wheat from the chaff.

Dew yew see if yew dunt! – just mark my words.

Ding o' the lug – customary punishment for a naughty boy – and a clip of the ear never did anyone any harm.

Dint they larn yew noffin at school? – Norfolk chastisement for being less than enlightened.

Dumpling-hunter – old-fashioned label for a hungry local preacher.

Dunt feel up tew a sight – a bit off colour.

Dunt git no further than Wensday – stupid sort.

Dunt yew be ser sorft – steady on, it must be my round.

Dunt yew peggarter orl his squit – useful advice to someone being taken in – 'I shouldn't pay regard to all his nonsense if I were you.'

Ent far wrong! – it's right!

Fair ter middlin' – stock response to inquiries about state of health.

Fare y'well, tergether – a fond goodbye. 'Tergether' refers to all present, whether singly or in a crowd. A young man was shocked when the father of his girlfriend bid them goodnight and said 'Time we all went ter bed, tergether!'

Flat as a cow's tad – cricket pitch after a good roll.

Git late earlier – nights are pulling in.

Gittin' suffin' dry – subtle hint from a drinker with an empty glass.

Git yew up an' cum down – Norfolk mother calling her lazy son.

Go-ter-meetin' clothes – best or Sunday garb. Known as 'becomes' in the old days.

Harvest festervals – large bloomers to inspire a chorus of 'All is safely gathered in'.

He'yer fa'r got a dickey, bor? – traditional question from one Norfolk person to another on meeting on strange territory. It means 'Has your father got a donkey, boy?' The correct reply from a fellow native is 'Yis, an' he want a fule ter roide'im, will yew cum?', meaning 'Yes, and he wants a fool to ride him, will you come?'.

He'yew got a loight, boy? – title of a song performed by the Singing Postman (Allan Smethurst) in the early 1960s. A natural successor in many ways to 'Ha'yer fa'r got a dickey, bor?'

He'yer got inny baccy onya enny onya? – call from a Norfolk man with empty pipe and pouch.

He cut sum grub inter him – tribute to a healthy eater.

He dun that a'parpuss – done deliberately, on purpose.

He mobbed a' rum'um – making a lot of fuss.

He wuz suffin' savidge – angry as well.

Hold yew hard! – hang on a moment, I could be right.

Hoss it up – lift it up.

Howen' an' mowen – just gossiping.

How yer gittin' on? – warmest of greetings.

Hello, my man or Hello, my woman – traditional Norfolk greeting for a baby in the pram on meeting in the street. Sometimes stretched to 'my little man' or 'my little woman' and often directed towards children holding hands with parents or grown-ups.

Hunnycart's on the way – posh folk call it the night soil collection vehicle. Other down-to-earth labels include the lavender cart or the violet wagon. One with a bell gloried in the name of humdinger.

I shall hatter keep a'dewin' – no alternative but to stick at it.

I weighed him up afore I say ennything – taking careful stock.

If his brearns wuz dynamite, they wunt blow his cap orff! – not too bright.

Jargon – what healthy Norfolk people do before breakfast – 'go a'jargon'.

Keep yar snout owt onnit – mind your own business, if you don't mind. Many thanks.

Keptathometogoataterin' – excuse in a note sent to a teacher by a Norfolk mother whose boy had been absent from school for several days.

Knockin' an' toppin' – the lot of the sugar beet worker before mechanisation. Often used to counter romantic notions about working on the land.

Know him ter see tew – know by sight if not by name.

Less hev sum loight on the job! – God at the Creation proving he likes the Norfolk dialect.

Like givin' a dickey wun oat! – a greedy type.

Lot of ole squit! – don't believe a word of it, even though it is being put over with such relish and colour.

Milestone inspector – a gentleman of the road.

My hart, he hallered! – such a noise.

My ole bewty! – as rich a greeting or description as a Norfolk native can muster. 'Ole partner' is nearly as good.

Mynd how yer go! – cheery farewell after all the formalities.

Never yew mynd where I live, dew yew cum an' see me – a subtle way of letting someone know you don't really want to associate.

Nobody dunt really want fer noffin' – poverty just isn't what it used to be!

Noffin' only the eyesight – pretty maybe, but of no material value.

No torkin', an' hev yer simptums riddy – notice in doctor's surgery.

No, there ent nun, not fer nobody – postman's reply on being asked if he has any letters for Sunnybrook Farm. Emphatic use of negative also found in 'Yew kin all go hoom, an' dunt none o' yew never cum back no more!'. Also on this trail – old chap grumbling because he can't find anyone to lend a hand: 'Thass the warst o' this here plearse – ent never nobody nowhere ter help nobody wi' noffin'.

Not tew bad – fair to middling.

On the sosh – just one of the colourful descriptions for something on the slant. Others include 'on the huh' and 'slantendicular'.

Ole Year's Nyte – New Year's Eve.

Puttin' har parts on – a young lady playing up, probably because her beau wants to play darts while she would prefer to go dancing.

Put yar considerin' cap on – just think about it.

Rafty ole weather – wet and windy.

Rare scolder of folk – a sizeable collection. 'A fair tidy few' probably means a gate of 20,000 at Carrow Road.

Reekun he see yew a'cummin! – blunt rejoinder to anyone complaining about being done.

Rum ole dew – a strange business, him being done like that.

Shud down the yard – outside toilet.

Shuttin' up tyme – getting dark.

Sinkers and swimmers – types of Norfolk dumplings.

Slow ole dry out terday – a wry summary of very wet weather.

Smurrin' wi' rain – heavy drizzle.

Sour as a wedge – bad-tempered sort.

Stand well clear o' yarself – important instructions to be followed on Bonfire Night.

Summer an' winter 'em fust – dominant characteristic of Norfolk people, especially where newcomers are concerned. Wait until you have their measure before accepting them.

Suffin' goin' abowt – Norfolk's most common ailment.

Swar'ston wynder – a black eye (Swardeston window).

Swedebasher – fairly amiable description of a Norfolk countryman, although a few have tried to turn it into a derogatory term.

Thass like this here – get ready for a lengthy explanation or yarn!

Thass orl a job – general exclamation, often accompanied by a sigh.

Thass throngy enow fer a tempest – a humid day with thunder in the air, storm brewing.

That dew crearze yer! – designed to get on one's nerves.

That'll larn yer! – serves you right, my good man, and let us hope the lesson has gone home.

The man wot put that thing tergether wunt no fule – labourer admiring a new self-binding machine in the harvest field.

Tew much book-larnin' – blatant shortage of practical knowledge.

There ent menny on'us left – mutual admiration society.

There he wuz – gorn! – rapid departure.

Thrippence short of a shillin' – not quite the whole ticket. Same as 'a few stick short of a bundle' and 'cupplar sandwidges short o' a picnic'.

Turned up queer and took and died – sad demise (remember 'queer' is ill).

Uppards an'downads – colourful description of sickness and diarrhoea.

Well, I'm still on the grownd – philosophical reply to inquiries about state of health. Also 'I'm still jammin' abowt!'.

'Wod she lay on yar shatt this mornin'? – gentle inquiry to a man late for work.

Wossitgotterdewwi'yew? – rebuke to anyone being too inquisitive.

Wunt a'went if Iyder known – wise after the event.

Yew'll git wrong – be prepared to get told off.

> Old George's wife died. The undertaker asked when the funeral would take place. 'Termorrer week' said George.
>
> 'Tomorrow week!' exclaimed the undertaker, 'That means a lapse of eight days. Any special reason for that?'.
>
> 'Thass like this here, marster' said George. 'We wuz married for 64 yeer, an' we allus reckoned when we wuz a' cortin' that if ever we git married we'd hev a quiet week on owr own. This is the only charnse I're hed, so now I'm a' gorter hev it!'

Litcham echo – agricultural dealer Abel Burton.

DO YOU KNOW?

County Facts

* The name 'Norfolk' is of Anglo-Saxon origin and means the place of the North folk ('Suffolk' – place of the South folk).

* Norfolk stands fourth in size among the counties of England, covering well over 2000 square miles. The Norfolk coastline stretches for nearly 100 miles.

* The Broads make up Britain's largest and most famous inland waterway with over 125 miles of navigable rivers and broads. They resulted from extensive digging for peat in the Middle Ages.

* In early days, Norfolk was dominated by the tribe of the Iceni. Their most famous leader was Boadicea (Boudicca) who led her people into bloody battle against the Romans in AD 61.

* The Domesday Book recorded Norfolk as the heaviest populated place in England in 1065.

* The Black Death was a terrible scourge in Norfolk in 1348, sweeping away a large proportion of the population of the towns and villages. More than 7000 people died in Great Yarmouth alone.

* King John, travelling from King's Lynn to Newark shortly before his death in October 1216, lost his baggage containing most of his treasures in the Wash.

* Kett's Rebellion of 1549 saw 20,000 Norfolk rebels led by Robert Kett, a tanner from Wymondham, rise up against what they saw as social and economic injustices, particularly the enclosure of common land. The rebellion lasted six weeks and ended in the Battle of Dussindale near Norwich. The ringleaders were executed.

* Norfolk mainly supported Parliament during the Civil War and became one of the six counties of the Eastern Association. King's Lynn remained staunchly Royalist, however, and Norwich was one of the first cities to welcome the return of Charles II.

* There are more villages in Norfolk with a Saxon church than in any other county. Round towers are common and of nearly 180 in England, 119 are in Norfolk.

* Norfolk has over 24,000 recorded archaeological sites, and 500 of them are protected by legislation.

* There are over 200 deserted villages in Norfolk, but most sites have been destroyed by ploughing. The earthworks at Godwick provide one of the best surviving examples in the county and the only one open to the public. First settled in late Saxon times, Godwick was inhabited until the 17th century and remained a separate parish until the early 19th century when it was incorporated in the parish of Tittleshall.

* There used to be 860 windmills and 100 wind pumps in Norfolk. About 50 are still standing more or less complete while many others are picturesque ruins. The corn mill at Sutton, near Stalham, is thought to be the tallest surviving windmill in Britain. It has nine floors.

* North Elmham was the seat of a Saxon bishop from AD 631 to 1071 before the bishopric moved first to Thetford and then, in 1096, to Norwich. Part of the stone Saxon throne is still preserved in Norwich Cathedral. In 1388 Henry Despenser, Bishop of Norwich, obtained a licence to convert the old North Elmham Cathedral into a country retreat for hunting. Nearly all the remaining external walls belong to the old monastic building.

* Castle Acre, with its great priory, castle and church, is an inspiring monument to medieval England. The castle remains are from the 13th century and include the flint and stone Bailey Gate which still guards the entrance to the market place. The village contains the earliest and most important Cluniac ruins in England and provides the finest monastic remains in East Anglia.

* Peddars Way is a long-distance path from Knettishall in Suffolk to Cromer on the North Norfolk coast. It follows the ancient Peddars Way track through Breckland to the coast at Holme, and has been extended from there along the coast to Cromer, a total of 65 miles.

* Weavers Way is a 15-mile route for walkers and cyclists between Blickling and Stalham, with extensions from Blickling to Cromer and from Stalham to Yarmouth through Broadland. The walk takes its name from the important weaving industry which used to flourish in the area.

* Poppyland is the name given to an area of the North Norfolk coast between Cromer and Sidestrand by journalist Clement Scott, who 'discovered' it towards the end of the last century. London's literary and artistic society made tracks for Poppyland after Scott's articles in the Daily Telegraph.

* Wayland Wood, near Watton, is one of the few areas of medieval woodland to survive in Norfolk. According to legend it was the setting for the story of the Babes in the Wood.

* Breckland lies partly in Norfolk and partly in Suffolk. It amounts to some 400 square miles. Large flint-strewn open fields and derelict areas known locally as Brecks induced historian and naturalist William George Clarke to give the region the name of Breckland in 1894.

* At Cockley Cley, near Swaffham, an Iceni village destroyed when the Romans marched into Norfolk after the defeat of Boadicea, has been effectively reconstructed in a wide valley shadowed by dark pines. .

* Grimes Graves Neolithic flint mines, made up of over 300 pits and shafts, cover about 34 acres at Weeting in Breckland. Flints were used as cutting tools more than 4000 years ago. The site is now under the protection of English Heritage and two of the fully excavated pits are open to the public.

* Houghton Hall, considered by many to be Norfolk's finest house, was built by Sir Robert Walpole, Great Britain's first Prime Minister, in 1721. In 1860 Houghton Hall was rejected as a possible home for the Prince of Wales in favour of Sandringham.

* Pensthorpe Waterfowl Park and Nature Reserve, near Fakenham, was created from flooded gravel workings. Gravel extraction took place between 1974 and 1979. From 1982 the pits were carefully restored as a nature reserve of 200 acres.

* The University of East Anglia was opened in Earlham, on the outskirts of Norwich, in 1963. Norwich City Hall was opened in 1938 by King George VI, and Norfolk County Hall was opened by Queen Elizabeth II in 1968. The Queen Mother opened the Royal Norfolk Regiment Museum in Norwich in 1990.

* There are seven places named Norwich and six Norfolks in the USA. You will find Norwich in Connecticut, Kansas, New York State (2), Vermont (2) and Long Island. There's also one in Ontario, Canada. You'll find Norfolk in Virginia (2), Maryland, Massachusetts, Nebraska and New York State.

* The Dutch engineer Cornelius Vermuyden built the first sluice at Denver, near Downham Market, in 1651 as part of a scheme to drain the fenlands owned by the Duke of Bedford. The oldest surviving sluice was built in 1843. Alongside is the Great Denver Sluice, opened in 1964.

* Worstead was once the prosperous centre for the manufacture of high-quality cloth, introduced by Flemish emigres and made of tightly knitted yarn. The church of St. Mary's is a legacy of Worstead's former riches, and the splendid church of St. Mary's at nearby Tunstead is another product of wool wealth.

* An important date in Norfolk's transport history is July 29th, 1845. The simultaneous opening of the Brandon and Norwich Railway and the Eastern Counties Railway extension from Newport to Brandon linked Norwich (Trowse) with London (Shoreditch) for the first time.

* The Norfolk Wherry Trust was formed in 1949 to preserve for posterity an example of the Norfolk trading wherry. The last wherry built was The Ella in 1912. They were forced into major decline by fast and convenient transport on road and rail. In 1949 the Wherry Albion was bought, refitted and rerigged, and still sails to this day. The sight of a black sail over Broadland remains one of the most evocative in Norfolk.

* Lord Nelson, Norfolk's most famous son, was born at Burnham Thorpe on September 29th, 1758. His father was the local Rector.

* The Norfolk Rural Life Museum at Gressenhall, near East Dereham, was once a workhouse. The 'House of Industry' was built in 1776. The Union, as it was known locally, continued in use until 1976, latterly as Beech House, an old people's home. All aspects of rural life since the 18th century are imaginatively displayed in the museum.

* Saint Walstan is Norfolk's patron saint of agriculture. Born in 961 at Bawburgh, near Norwich, he gave up his inheritance to live the simple life of a worker on the land. On May 30th, 1016, began a story which is now a legend after Bishop Algar of Elmham took the burial service and declared Walstan a saint. The waters of St. Walstan's Well at Bawburgh became renowned for their curative properties for humans and animals alike.

The City Beat

* Norwich Cathedral, built by the Normans from 1096 onwards, is one of the most beautiful in England. The 315-foot spire is second only to Salisbury in height. Bishop Herbert de Losinga laid the cathedral's foundation stone and by the time he died in 1119 his church was built as far as the twisted pillars.

* Norwich Castle dates from the 12th century but it was refaced in 1834. It stands on a 40-foot high artificial mound surrounded by a moat. The castle houses a museum showing the natural history and geology of the region as well as archaeological discoveries.

* Norwich was the second city in the country after London in the 17th and 18th centuries.

* The Norwich city wall was started in 1294 and completed in 1343. The walls were about two and a half miles long in all, stood 20-foot high and contained 37,000 tonnes of masonry.

* Elizabeth I visited Norwich for a five-day stay in 1578. She was entertained and feasted at the Guildhall, Bishop's Palace and by various city guilds.

* Gurney Bank was formed in Norwich in 1775 and amalgamated with Barclays in 1896 to grow into one of the leading banks in the world.

* Norwich's Theatre Royal stands on the site of its two predecessors. The first was designed and built by Thomas Ivory in 1757 and the second in 1826. The present building dates from 1935 after a disastrous fire. The Theatre first opened on January 31st, 1758, with 'The Way of the World' by William Congreve. The following week a presentation of Shakespeare's Henry V was enjoyed by a patriotic audience. It was during the Seven Years War between England and France, and the play was sub-titled 'The Victory of the English over the French'.

* Ber Street in Norwich was known for many years as 'Blood and Guts Street' from the high number of butchers shops and slaughterhouses near the old cattle market.

* The Bethel Hospital in Norwich is the oldest psychiatric hospital in Britain still being used for its original purpose. It was built in 1713 by Mary Chapman. She died in 1724, but the hospital continued to pioneer methods of curing mental illness.

* It used to be said that Norwich had a pub for every day of the year and a church for every Sunday. In fact, in medieval times there were 56 parish churches within the city walls.

* Jeremiah Colman, mustard magnate and kindly employer, moved the business from Stoke Holy Cross outside the city to Carrow in Norwich – and Colman has been the best known name in the mustard business ever since. Jeremiah and his wife started the Carrow social welfare scheme in 1856 and their practical welfare work was crowned with the beginning of a nursing service. In 1938 the company was amalgamated with Reckitts.

* Actor and dancer Will Kemp is famous for dancing from London to Norwich in 1559. The actual dancing took nine days but the entire journey lasted about four weeks. His name is kept to the fore in Norfolk by Kemp's Men, a Morris dancing group.

* Jenny Lind, known as the Swedish Nightingale because of her

lovely voice, founded the children's hospital in Norwich which bears her name. Two concerts she gave in the city in 1849 raised over 1200 which she wanted to be used to establish some new and lasting charity for the poor. The Jenny Lind Infirmary For Sick Children was founded in 1853.

* Louis Marchesi founded the international Round Table movement in Norwich in 1927. By the time Round Table held their 40th anniversary luncheon the movement had spread to 28 countries. It was the last public appearance for 'Mark' as he became known, for he died in December 1968.

* Founder and father-figure of the world famous Norwich School of Painting, John Crome was a fine technician in both oils and watercolour. The Norwich Society was formed in 1803 and that prepared the ground for the Norwich School of Painters which was to survive three generations of local artists. It was the first exhibition by a society of artists other than those held in London.

* Thomas Bignold, who moved to Norwich from Kent in 1783, founded the Norwich Union a few years later, and it became one of the largest insurance organisations in the world. The Bignold name continued to dominate Norwich Union until the retirement of Sir Robert Bignold in 1964.

* Nugent Monck founded the Maddermarket Theatre in Norwich in 1921. The former Roman Catholic chapel was transformed into an Elizabethan theatre. During one period, Monck produced every one of Shakespeare's plays. It is a tradition that all Maddermarket actors remain anonymous.

* Luke Hansard, who went to London to become official printer of all debates in the House of Commons, was born in Norwich in 1752.

* An outstanding surgeon of his day, William Fellowes founded the Norfolk and Norwich Hospital in 1771. Fellowes subscribed the first £1000 of the £13,000 building fund and he laid the foundation stone.

* Chief Constable of Norwich for nearly 27 years, John Dain founded the Lads' Club in the city in 1918 to give some purpose to working-class youths who were aimlessly roaming the streets.

* Dragon Hall in Norwich is the only medieval merchant's trading hall known to survive in Western Europe. It was built by Robert Toppes in the 15th century, and is now maintained by the Norfolk and Norwich Heritage Trust.

Round the Towns

ATTLEBOROUGH

Gaymers' cider-making plant was built near the railway at Attleborough in 1896 and soon became the largest employer in the town. Before that Gaymers had been making cider at their plant in the nearby village of Banham since at least the 1700s.

* King Edward VII paid a brief visit to Attleborough on October 26th, 1909, with thousands turning out to greet their monarch. He was visiting the Earl of Albermarle at his Quidenham home and decided to pay an unofficial call in town. Next day the King travelled to Norwich for the first royal visit to the city since Charles II in 1671.

* It is surprising to find the Norman tower of Attleborough parish church at the east end of the building. The tower stood at the west end of the original Norman church but when a monastery was established here in 1386 a new nave was built west of the tower for use by the laity. At the Dissolution the Norman church was pulled down.

* Attleborough used to have a turkey fair every year, after which the flocks of turkeys were walked to London along the Great Post Road, now the A11.

* The war memorial in the middle of Attleborough commemorates those who died in the Battle of Inkerman (1856) in the Crimean War.

AYLSHAM

Aylsham is recorded as 'Elesham' in the Domesday Survey completed by the Normans in 1086. In 1372 Edward III granted Aylsham Lancaster, with other manors and estates in Norfolk, to his son John of Gaunt. As a result it became a place of considerable importance, for John of Gaunt established here his court of the Duchy of Lancaster for the whole of Norfolk. Even before this time Aylsham had become widely known as the centre of linen manufacture in the county.

* The place still called the Buttlands is where the men of Aylsham regularly practised with their bows on a Sunday. They also instructed their sons in acquiring skills with the long bow, such a deadly weapon when used during the victorious battles on the Continent.

* Aylsham Parish Church is believed to have been built by John of Gaunt when he was lord of the manor in about 1380. In the churchyard is the tomb of outstanding 19th century landscape gardener Humphrey Repton.

* Executed for high treason in 1723, Christopher Layer, the only militant Jacobite Norfolk produced, is remembered with a plaque on a house in the town.

* Born over a shop on the corner of Aylsham market place in 1825, Joseph Thomas Clover was probably the first full-time consulting anaesthetist in England.

CROMER

Part of Cromer's early history is hidden beneath the sea. Over 600 years ago there stood beyond Cromer the village of Shipden. It was swept away by coast erosion, but somewhere out towards the end of the pier there is a mass of flint called Church Rock – and tradition says that it is what is left of Shipden church tower.

* Cromer's present pier was opened in 1901 – and has never made a penny profit. The annual summer show in the Pavilion Theatre at the end of the pier claims to be the last remaining genuine show of its kind. The first mention of a pier in Cromer comes from 1391.

* The earliest light for mariners was a fire burning on a platform halfway up Cromer church tower. In 1719 a brick lighthouse was built on the hills to the east of the town. When in 1832 a big cliff-fall threatened the lighthouse another was built further inland. This is the one that stands there today.

* Henry Blogg, Cromer lifeboat coxswain for 38 years, won more medals than any other lifeboatman. Three times he won the gold medal – the lifeboatman's VC – and four times the silver medal. Other awards included the George Cross and the British Empire Medal. During his years of service the Cromer boat went out 387 times and saved 873 lives. Blogg retired in 1947 after 53 years of service in all.

* Cromer Museum was set up in a terrace of five Victorian fishermen's cottages, one of which has been furnished as it would have been just before the First World War.

DISS

Diss takes its name from the Old English 'dic' meaning a ditch or a pond, a most appropriate name given that the town is built around a six-acre mere or lake.

* Sir John Betjeman, the people's Poet Laureate, voted Diss his favourite English town, and the man reckoned to be the very first Poet Laureate, John Skelton, was rector of Diss for 25 years. Mary Wilson, wife of former Prime Minister Harold Wilson, lived in Diss as a child.

* Diss Fair evidently started in 1185 when permission was granted by royal charter to the lord of the manor. Cock Street Green became the fair's home from the mid-15th century, a tradition that continued until 1872.

* One reason for the survival of quaint old-time houses in the town is that Diss, unlike most English towns, escaped a major fire in Tudor times.

DOWNHAM MARKET

Downham was once a sizable inland port but the railways and a new canal cut off the town from the river.

* Much of the town is built of carrstone from nearby quarries. The market place is dominated by the Gothic cast-iron clock, Big Ben in miniature, given to the town in 1878 by James Scott.

* George Manby, whose many inventions included the rocket life-saving apparatus, and Horatio Nelson, destined to become the most honoured naval leader Britain has known, both spent part of their schooldays in Downham.

* After his defeat at Naseby, King Charles I visited Downham on May Day 1646. He was disguised as a clergyman and on his way to surrender to the Scottish army at Newark. He stayed overnight at an inn where the present Swan Hotel stands.

EAST DEREHAM

William Cowper (1731–1800) is buried at East Dereham parish church. He wrote some of our most famous hymns and broke fresh poetic grounds despite frequent bouts of insanity. George Borrow, writer and champion of the gipsy way of life, was born at Dumpling Green in the town in 1803.

* There was a time when you could travel to any part of the country by rail from Dereham. The Beeching Axe changed all that in 1964 when the Dereham–Wells section closed. The Dereham–Lynn line went in 1968, and the last passenger service from Dereham to Norwich ran in 1970. The railway came to Dereham in 1846 when the Norfolk Railway Company built a single track from Wymondham.

* The firm of Hobbies was started in Dereham in 1897 by J. H. Skinner, who had started publication of Hobbies Weekly two years before. Hobbies became the largest employer in the town and its products, mainly fretwork tools and materials, were sold all over the world. The firm went into decline and closed in 1969.

* David Fisher built the Theatre Royal in Dereham in 1812 and based his travelling theatrical company in the town. It was later used for concerts, dances, boxing tournaments and other social events. It became a canteen for troops during the First World War, and in the 1960s it was used as additional classroom accommodation for the National Junior School. In 1977 a group of Dereham doctors demolished the old theatre and erected the town's first purpose-built surgery on the site.

* Bishop Bonner's Cottages in Dereham were built in 1502 and now house the local antiquarian society's museum. Edmund Bonner was Dereham's rector from 1534 until 1540. He became Bishop of London and gained notoriety for burning about 200 people at the stake during the heresy trials in Mary Tudor's reign.

FAKENHAM

Fakenham's 19th century gasworks have been restored for visitors. The town's museum of gas and local history provides the only surviving example in England of the small horizontal retort hand-fired gasworks. The works were closed in 1965.

* Fakenham was granted a market in 1250, and in 1609 its importance was recognised by the church. The Bishop of Norwich wrote to the Rectors of Fakenham and 'Rainham' requesting they furnish a rota of preachers for the market.

* The Norfolk Railway reached Fakenham in 1848. Nine years later the line was extended to Wells, giving Fakenham an excuse for a public holiday. In 1862, the Great Eastern Railway took over this line as well as the line from East Dereham to Fakenham. The Lynn and Fakenham Railway reached the town in 1880 and then continued to Melton Constable.

* Printing was Fakenham's main industry for many years. The first recorded printers in the town were Stewardsons, who were printing stagecoach posters at the turn of the 1800s and who continued until the 1960s.

* Fakenham's longest-running fair was the Sheep Fair originally

held in Kipton about four miles away. It disappeared in the 1840s but was revived on Hempton Green in 1848 and continued until 1969.

* Pudding Norton also hosts an event with the 'Fakenham' label. This is the horseracing first held on a purpose-built course in 1906 when the West Norfolk Hunt moved its steeplechase from East Winch. Six Fakenham race meetings are now held each year.

* Born in Fakenham in 1851, John Cousins Garrood was responsible for many new ideas regarding cycle construction. He was the first to use tubular construction for the forks and he also made use of ball bearings. There is a road named after him on the town's industrial estate.

GREAT YARMOUTH

From the earliest settlement, Yarmouth's street pattern has been based on a unique plan, a system of urban development not to be found in any other town in the country. For nine hundred years the old town – that part within the medieval wall – was laid out in ranks of buildings separated by three north-east streets and nearly 150 east-west 'rows' – the famous Yarmouth Rows.

* The Yarmouth Roads, a safe anchorage, are formed by a sandbank three miles due east of the town which acts as a natural breakwater. At low tide Scroby Sands may be seen quite easily. It was in 1580 that the sandbank really became dry and it was soon a favourite resort for summer picnics.

* After draining the valleys of Norfolk and Suffolk, the three great rivers, Waveney, Yare and Bure, combine in one large lake known as Breydon Water just west of Yarmouth. Breydon, with its broad sheets of water, shallow flats and surrounding marshes, is as rich in water fowl and waders as any district in the country.

* The military first organised horseracing in Yarmouth on the South Denes in the 18th century. From 1810 regular meetings were held there until the present racecourse was built on the North Denes in 1922. Nelson's Monument, built by public subscription in

1819, stands 144 feet high with Britannia on top. It was built in the centre of the original racecourse.

* The most important post-war development at Yarmouth came in the early 1960s when it was made the first base for oil and gas exploration in the North Sea. The first drilling rig, 'Mr Cap', started operations off the Norfolk coast in 1964, and engineering and servicing companies set up base in the town. Gas was found in 1965 and by the end of the decade there were 27 rigs working in the southern North Sea, most of them supported by tugs, supply vessels and survey vessels from Yarmouth – the largest offshore base in Europe.

* The Scots fisher fleet arrived in Yarmouth each October from 1912. The following year 1163 boats caught 800,000 crans of herring, a cran being 1132 fish. By the late 1950s catches had declined to around 20,000 crans. Only five drifters came in 1968 and none at all the year after. Gutting and packing was nearly all done by girls.

* Yarmouth's three piers have been destroyed, damaged and modified many times over the centuries. Oldest is the jetty dating from 1560 and where Nelson landed twice. The Wellington Pier opened in 1854 and the Britannia in 1858.

* In 1261 Henry III gave permission for the building of the town wall at Yarmouth. Work began in 1285 but it wasn't completed until about 1400. The original wall was built of flint with a brick and rubble core, backed by a brick arcade carrying a wall walk. The gates were demolished to allow road widening but almost two thirds of the wall survives in whole or part, including eleven towers and turrets. This makes it one of the most complete medieval walls in England.

* In 1984 the Yarmouth District General Hospital, situated in Gorleston, was renamed the James Paget Hospital after the leading surgeon and medical authority of his day. James Paget was born in Yarmouth in 1814 and died in 1899. His family had been in the town for 200 years and his father, Samuel, was mayor in 1817.

* Anna Sewell, whose only book, 'Black Beauty', became one of the

world's best sellers, was born in Yarmouth in 1820. Her birthplace in the north-east corner of the market place, nestling in the shadow of the parish church, has been used as a restaurant and tea-room in recent years.

HARLESTON

Harleston's famous stone is in the alleyway connecting Broad Street with The Thoroughfare. It is of glacial origin and its top contains a cup-like hole, probably used to disinfect money to be used at the market during the time of the Great Plague. The Harleston stone is thought to have been used by King Harold for his proclamation and by his herald to issue orders to the troops. The stone was also used over the years for horse-mounting.

* Harleston's stocking factory opened in 1912, with Mr and Mrs William Cumming as proprietors. At first the factory specialised in making ladies' stockings, but with the advent of the First World War contracts came for the manufacture of the famous army grey socks for soldiers fighting in the front line. Looms were driven by a portable steam engine. The factory gradually ran down after the end of the war.

HOLT

Gresham's School at Holt was founded as a Free Grammar School in the 1550s, and continued as such until 1900 when Headmaster G. W. S. Howson transformed it into the public school still flourishing today. There were boarders before 1630, when the fees were £7 a year for a boarder. Famous former pupils of more recent times include W. H. Auden and Benjamin Britten.

* Holt Hall, a residential education centre, became the emergency crash centre after an air disaster over the town in August, 1968. Two RAF aircraft, a Victor tanker from RAF Marham and a Canberra from RAF Germany, collided over Holt and all seven crew members were killed.

* Holt Country Park, on the B1149 Norwich road as you leave the

town, is owned and managed by North Norfolk District Council. Bought in 1979, this area has a colourful history, records showing a racecourse running from the Norwich road to the Hempstead road from the early 1700s to 1810.

* Holt livestock market closed in 1960.

HUNSTANTON

Hunstanton has the unique distinction of being the only resort on the east coast to face west. It takes newcomers some time to get used to the apparent phenomenon of seeing the sun set over the sea instead of over land.

* Around 1840 there was nothing between Old Hunstanton and Heacham. Henry Styleman Le Strange, Lord of the Manor and heriditary Lord High Admiral of the Wash, decided to develop the area south of the old village as a sea bathing resort. The town was described as 'the poor man's St. Moritz' while water from a spring at nearby Ringstead was said to be of better quality than that of Harrogate.

* Hunstanton's cliffs consist of a thin layer of red chalk sandwiched between white chalk and brown sandstone, the latter known as carrstone and used in the building of many local houses.

* The railway came to Hunstanton in 1862. It survived the original Beeching cuts but was closed in 1969. In 1863 a train was derailed on the King's Lynn-Hunstanton line after colliding with a bull. Seven people were killed.

* Hunstanton pier, built in 1870 and measuring 830 feet in length, was destroyed in a heavy storm on the night of January 11th, 1978.

KING'S LYNN

King's Lynn was originally called Bishop's Lynn. It was founded by Herbert de Losinga, the first Bishop of Norwich, in about 1100. The King seized the town in 1536.

* The Theatre Royal in Lynn was opened in 1815 and modernised in 1904. It was burned down in 1936, a cinema emerging on the same site three years later.

* One of Lynn's most delightful buildings, the Customs House, was built in 1683 by local merchant Henry Bell. He was twice mayor of Lynn. It was originally used as an exchange, and a statue of Charles II stands in a niche over the King Street entrance.

* The Carnegie Public Library in Lynn was built of carrstone and brick and named after the Scottish-born American millionaire Andrew Carnegie, who provided the funds. He opened it on May 18th, 1905.

* Another famous Lynn landmark is Our Lady's Chapel at Red Mount, built in 1485 in the form of an octagon. It was intended as a resting place for pilgrims on their way to the holy shrine at Walsingham.

* The Lynn to Hunstanton railway was opened in 1862. Wolferton station was built to serve the Sandringham Estate. When the last train ran in 1966 the little station had received over 640 royal trains since it opened. It is now a private house and museum.

* The annual civic ceremony of the grand opening of the King's Lynn Mart is held on St. Valentine's Day. The mart or fair takes place on the Tuesday Market Place and runs for two weeks.

* Among famous people born in Lynn – writer Fanny Burney (born 1752); Margery Kempe, whose life is the first known autobiography in English literature (born 1373); explorer George Vancouver (born 1757); and John Mason, who founded the state of New Hampshire in USA (born 1586).

NORTH WALSHAM

Built in the middle of the 16th century to replace an earlier crumbling construction, North Walsham's Market Cross was almost completely destroyed in the great fire of 1600. It was rebuilt two years later. Ownership passed to the Ecclesiastical Commissioners in 1830, who later sold it to the town together with the market rights. It was extensively renovated in 1899 when a clock and bell were installed by the Urban District Council. During raids by German aircraft in 1942 the weather vane was blown off by a blast from a heavy explosive bomb.

* The parish church of St. Nicholas overshadows North Walsham's medieval market place – and its tower has been a ruin since 1724. The tower was built in three stages after work started early in the 14th century. On Friday, May 15th, 1724, the town held its Ascension Day Fayre and the bells were rung for many hours. The following morning, without any warning, the tower fell. A tower rebuilding fund was started in 1749, but there's no evidence of any real construction work. The last major fall came in 1836 amid extreme gales. In 1939 the ruined tower was considered dangerous and £550 was spent on making it secure in the hope it might be rebuilt one day. In 1972 the new choir vestry and practice room was built into the tower.

* The North Walsham to Dilham Canal was formally opened on Tuesday, August 29th, 1826. It started at Wayford Bridge in Dilham, where it connected with the River Ant, and then passed through Worstead, Westwick, Honing and Crostwick Hall, leaving North Walsham and Suffield Hall on the west and proceeding to Witton Park and to its termination at Antingham, a distance of seven miles. After the First World War traffic from the mills along the canal fell dramatically and continued to decline. In 1935 commercial navigation along the water course ceased altogether.

SHERINGHAM

Sheringham is mentioned in the Domesday Book under the name of Sillingham. It was given by William the Conqueror, with other lands in Norfolk, to William Scholes as a reward for services rendered at the Battle of Hastings.

* In Upper Sheringham, the great landscape gardener Humphrey Repton created what he called his favourite park around Sheringham Hall. When Repton began work in 1812 he found a site

already so well wooded and full of natural delights he was able to achieve his desires with minimal change, but he did plant newly-imported species of rhododendron and azalea. Repton's client was Abbot Upcher, squire of Sheringham. On the death of Thomas Upcher in 1985 the estate was purchased by the National Trust.

SWAFFHAM

The privilege of holding a market at Swaffham was granted during the reign of King John in about 1214. It meant the market had some legal protection against other markets being set up in nearby villages. Until relatively recently the rights to hold the market and fairs were held solely by the Lord of the Manor of Swaffham, but now the town council administers the whole market, the biggest Saturday market in the region.

* Building of the present Swaffham parish church began in 1454 on the site of a parish church which had collapsed. John Botewright was the rector responsible for rebuilding the church, and he also made a gift of land known as 'The Campingland' to the people of Swaffham in 1463 for sport, military drill and 'honest games'.

* Swaffham's present Market Cross was built in 1783 for George, Earl of Orford, grandson of Sir Robert Walpole. It was also known as the Butter Cross for trading in butter went on under the roof of the building. The Earl of Orford founded Swaffham Coursing Club in 1786, the first such club in the country and still in existence.

* During this century three lay preachers from Swaffham Methodist Church have become Members of Parliament – William Taylor, Sidney Dye and Albert (later Lord) Hilton.

THETFORD

Thomas Paine, the most outstanding political writer and radical thinker of the late 18th century, was born in Thetford in 1737. For many years after his death he was disowned by his native town, but in 1964 he was honoured with a gilded statue paid for by the Thomas Paine Foundation of America.

* Thetford was the fastest-growing town in Britain in the 1970s. Overspill from London and the new industry which accompanied the influx of population drastically changed the character of the town. Thetford more than quadrupled its population between 1951 and 1981. It was in May, 1957, that Thetford Borough Council and the London County Council signed the formal agreement with the first overspill tenants moving in just under two years later.

* Thetford's Castle Hill is one of the highest earthworks of its kind in the country. It stands 80 feet high and is about 1000 feet in circumference at the base. The Normans constructed many similar earthworks during their conquest of England. Castle Hill was probably last used for military purposes late in the 11th century.

* The Burrell Engineering Works dominated Thetford for many years. Joseph, William and James Burrell started to produce agricultural implements in the early 1800s. Charles Burrell (1817–1906) began the production of a portable steam engine in 1848 and the traction engine was exported all over the world. The works closed in the late 1920s. The Charles Burrell Museum, located in the former paint shop, opened in 1990.

* Thetford's Bell Inn was a popular coaching and posting inn on the road between Norwich and London. The last horse-drawn Royal Mail coach between the two cities passed through Thetford in 1846.

WATTON

The Watton Show, known for many years as the Wayland Agricultural Show, started in the 1790s as a show of cottage garden and home produce, There were a few classes for cattle and farm crops by the start of the 1800s. The character of the show changed after the Second World War with large entries in horse-jumping and goat classes. Now it attracts many commercial stands that have nothing to do with agriculture – just like the Royal Norfolk Show.

* The Thetford to Watton railway line opened in October, 1869. Six years later the line was extended to Swaffham. The line was called the 'Crab and Winkle' by locals.

* Building work on the RAF station at Watton was sufficiently advanced for it to be opened on January 4th, 1939. On the outbreak of war eight months later two squadrons of Blenheim bombers, Nos 21 and 82, formed No 79 Wing. The first American airmen arrived in July 1943 to maintain, service and repair all aircraft in the Second Air Division. It was Second Air Division who occupied 14 bases in Norfolk flying B24 Liberators. At the height of operations 6600 Americans were at Watton, about three times the town's population at the time.

* In May, 1980, a number of empty houses on the RAF station at Watton became homes for 65 Vietnamese refugees, so-called 'Boat People'. Many Watton residents, along with people from the nearby village of Carbrooke, gave furniture, clothing and time to set up the rehabilitation centre.

WELLS

The name of Wells is derived from the fact that it used to tap the springs of fresh water held by the underlying chalk on which it is built. Many houses relied on their own wells, often inside the house itself, for their water supplies.

* Wells Cottage Hospital was built by the tenants of the Holkham Estate as the Wells and District Memorial Hospital in memory of their 'guv'nor', the second Earl of Leicester. It opened in 1910 with eight beds and an operating theatre was added in 1926.

* The parish church of St. Nicholas at Wells is a reconstruction. The old building was struck by lightning and largely destroyed in 1879. Among those buried in the churchyard is John Fryer, who served as Master of the Bounty, the ship at the heart of the most famous mutiny in maritime history. Fryer died in 1817 at the age of 63.

* Sydney Long, who founded the Norfolk Naturalists' Trust in 1926, was born in Wells, son of the local doctor.

WYMONDHAM

The Market Cross in the centre of Wymondham was built in 1616 and served for many years until the First World War as a public reading-room and library. Wymondham has more listed buildings than any similar-sized town in the county, most of them built after the disastrous fire of 1615.

* The charming old-world thoroughfare of Damgate in Wymondham was once on the main Norwich to London road. Many weavers lived there in the late 18th and early 19th centuries.

* The Wymondham Bridewell was founded in 1785 as a place where offenders could be rehabilitated as well as imprisoned. The town's old Bridewell stood on the same site as the present building and it is likely some of the dungeon-like cells were incorporated in the new building. Sir Thomas Beevor, a local magistrate, was responsible for the new Bridewell.

> A couple of American servicemen were waiting for a train. They kept on telling the old Norfolk porter they had bigger and faster trains back home. They were just about to elaborate when a fast train to Yarmouth raced through, hauled by a Britannia class locomotive. 'Gee, buddy, what was that?' asked one of the Americans. 'Oh' said the porter, 'That wuz ole Tom dewin' a bit o' shuntin'!'.

Sticking to the task.

First and Last

The first railway in Norfolk was opened on April 30th, 1844, covering a 20-mile stretch from Norwich to Great Yarmouth. A train of 14 vehicles was assembled behind one of the little engines, which took 50 minutes for the journey to the coast. It returned later that day to Norwich in 44 minutes – not far short of the present journey time.

* Britain's first modern beet sugar factory was built on the banks of the River Yare at Cantley, about 12 miles east of Norwich, and opened for business on November 11th, 1912. It was largely due to the vision and determination of Dutchman Jerald van Rossum that the factory was built.

* The 300-year tradition of Mayor of Great Yarmouth was ended in January, 1991, with claims that abolishing the role would save money and that a council chairman could do just as efficient a job. Labour's Bill Dougal was the last mayor.

* Local television output began in 1959. BBC Television from All Saints Green in Norwich first went out on October 5th. Anglia Television, who had converted Norwich Agricultural Hall into their headquarters, started broadcasting three weeks later on October 27th.

* BBC Radio Norfolk was launched in September, 1980. Radio Broadland, the county's first commercial station, first went on the air in October, 1984.

* The Norfolk police force was founded in 1839. The county magistrates took the bold and hotly-contested decision to form one of the first professional police forces for rural areas in the country. A force of 133 officers were described by an opponent as a 'movable rambling police which no-one will ever know where to find'. As it grew the county constabulary absorbed the separate professional forces which once existed at Thetford, King's Lynn, Yarmouth and Norwich.

* Ethel Colman became the first woman Lord Mayor of Norwich in 1923. In the same year Dorothy Jewson became the first Norwich woman Member of Parliament.

* William Faden published what is thought to be the first large-scale map of Norfolk in 1797. Geographer to King George III and the Prince of Wales, he published many other maps during his career.

* The first Eastern Daily Press – or Eastern Counties Daily Press as it was called – appeared on the streets on October 10th, 1870. It cost one penny and the front page was devoted entirely to advertisements. The word 'Counties' was dropped from the title after six months. The Eastern Evening News was launched in 1882.

* The first Zeppelin raid over England claimed two lives in Yarmouth on the night of January 19th, 1915. Martha Taylor, a 72-year-old spinster and 53-year-old shoemaker Samuel Smith were the first people killed in England by bombs from the air. Also killed that night at King's Lynn were 14-year-old Percy Goate and 26-year-old Alice Gazley.

* The first purpose-built cinema in East Anglia was The Gem at Great Yarmouth, completed in 1908. It is known today as the Windmill Theatre on the Golden Mile. It was in January, 1897, that George Gilbert introduced 'The Royal Cinematographe – The Animated Photographs' – presenting with marvellous accuracy scenes of everyday life' at the Agricultural Hall in Norwich.

* The first Thorpe railway station in Norwich was built in 1844 as the terminus for the Norwich-Yarmouth line. The present station was built in 1886.

* Caister-on-Sea claims to have established the first real holiday camp in England. In 1906 Fletcher Dodd opened his 'Socialist Camp' in the village, providing holidays for small groups from the East End of London. Dodd soon realised the potential of his idea; wooden chalets replaced tents and dining and entertainment halls were built. In 1924 a week's holiday cost two guineas inclusive of all meals and transport from the railway station.

* Probably the earliest agricultural show in Norfolk was the Holkham Sheep Shearings of 1778. Agricultural associations were formed in east and west Norfolk in 1825 and 1834 respectively. These amalgamated in 1847 to form the Norfolk Agricultural Association which was granted the 'Royal' prefix in 1907.

* The first Norfolk Agricultural Show was held in 1847 at Norwich Cricket Ground. After 1862 the Norfolk Show was held in a different town each year, but after the Second World War it became increasingly difficult to find sites large enough. Since 1954 all Royal Norfolk Shows have been held on the permanent site at Costessey.

* Norwich City Football Club's first match in Division One was at Carrow Road on Saturday August 12th, 1972. A crowd of 26,028 saw them draw 1–1 with Everton, Scotsman Jimmy Bone scoring the Canaries' first goal in the top flight.

* Norwich St. Edmund Rotary Club made history in August, 1991, when it was joined by the first woman member in East Anglia – Jacqui Lomas, director of finance and administration for Norfolk Police.

* In 1787 the 'First Fleet' of transported convicts set sail from Plymouth to found the colony of New South Wales in Australia. It included Henry Cabell and Susannah Holmes, who fell in love and conceived their first child while in Norwich Prison. Originally, only Susannah and her son were to be transported, but Henry was allowed to join them by direct intervention of the then Home Secretary, Lord Sydney. Tradition has it that Henry was the first man to set foot in the colony after wading ashore with the ship's captain on his shoulders.

* The first clergyman to be awarded the Victoria Cross settled in Norfolk after winning the honour in the Afghan War. James Adams held the living at Postwick, near Norwich, from 1887 to 1894 and then moved to Stow Bardolph in the Fens.

* Norfolk's first holder of the Victoria Cross was Private Henry Ward from Harleston. He joined the 78th Rosshire Buffs in 1843, and his claim to fame came during the Indian Mutiny with the revolt of the Bengal Army against the British.

* Writer and scholar Thomas Browne was the first to notice Norfolk had a dialect of its own. He spent much of his life in Norwich and his statue on Hay Hill in the city was unveiled in 1904. He was knighted by Charles II in 1671 as a steadfast Royalist famous for his antiquarian scholarship.

* Sheringham's Little Theatre is home to Britain's only surviving weekly repertory company, with a variety of plays for visitors and locals alike during the summer season.

* The last public execution to be held in Norwich was on April 21st, 1849. About 12,000 people saw James Bloomfield Rush, the notorious Stanfield Hall murderer, go to the scaffold in front of the castle.

* John Bowman was Norwich City Football Club's first professional manager. He was appointed in March, 1905, when City turned professional and joined the Southern League

Biggest and Best

Cromer's parish church tower is the highest in Norfolk apart from Norwich Cathedral – it soars 160 feet up. St Nicholas at Great Yarmouth is the largest parish church in the country. It was badly damaged by fire bombs in the last war.

* Holkham National Nature Reserve is the largest in England, extending over 10,000 acres of marshes, dunes and intertidal mudflats along nine miles of coast from Burnham Overy to Blakeney.

* Thetford Forest is the largest lowland forest in Britain, covering an area of 80 square miles and supplying about six per cent of the timber harvested by the Forestry Commission. Planting began in 1922.

* The Maid's Head Hotel in Norwich has challenged any hotel in Britain to produce a better record of continuous service – more than 700 years. No serious contender has come forward.

* The Paston Letters are the earliest great collection of family letters in English, spanning three generations of the family who took their name from the village where they lived near the northeast coast of Norfolk. The letters give an intimate picture of everyday life in the 15th century. Historian Francis Blomefield brought them to light in 1735 when he was invited to Oxnead. In the country house built by William Paston he found the precious letters among the ancient tomes, documents, boxes and ledgers.

* The Burston School Strike was the longest in English history. Started by children at the village school near Diss in April, 1914, when their teachers Tom and Kitty Higdon were dismissed, it went on until just before the Second World War. The strike school is now a museum.

* The highest point above mean sea-level in Norfolk is Piggs' Grave crossroads, Swanton Novers, at 331 feet. Roman Camp at Aylmerton, near Cromer, is next at 329 feet, with Pigg's Grave crossroads at Melton Constable and the Pretty Corner turning on the A148 near Sheringham in joint third on 322 feet.

Sporting File

The Norfolk County Cricket Club was formed on January 11th, 1827, at the Rampant Horse Inn, Norwich, with Lord Suffield as president. Norfolk's first inter-county match was played at East Dereham against Lincolnshire in July, 1828. The Lakenham Festival Week in Norwich started in 1881.

* Norfolk cricketers took part in the first Minor Counties Championship in 1895 and headed the table in that first year, bracketed with Durham and Worcestershire. Norfolk won the title outright in 1905, 1910 and 1913.

* In 1815 a cricket team from Fakenham, Hempton and Walsingham were all out for nought against the combined forces of Brisley, Dunham and Litcham. This may help explain why it wasn't until 1883 that Fakenham took the solo plunge and formed the town club.

* The social importance of 18th century Swaffham is underlined by the fact that in 1797 a cricket match was played in the town between 33 men of Norfolk and an England eleven. England won. The pitch was in a clearing in the middle of the three-mile racecourse. This was said to rival Newmarket and was in existence from at least 1628, making it one of the oldest in the country. Racing finished in Swaffham in about 1825.

* The most celebrated cricket match staged in Norfolk was at Old Buckenham in June, 1921. Lionel Robinson, an Australian trying hard to become an English gentleman, persuaded the Australians to play the second match of their tour on his estate. It was seen as a full dress-rehearsal for the forthcoming Tests, and there was a great pilgrimage from all parts of Norfolk and adjoining counties to see Jack Hobbs and his colleagues take on the tourists. Rain cut play to 15 minutes on the first day, but a crowd of nearly 10,000 poured in on the second day to see Hobbs score 85 in what he later described as the best knock of his career. The game petered out into a draw as the rain returned – but 'The Private Test Match' stands out as one of the biggest sporting events in Norfolk history.

* King Edward VII had a great love of racehorses. The most famous was Persimmon, who won many Classic races including the Derby in 1896, the St Leger and the Ascot Gold Cup. In 1903 the Jockey Club gave the Sandringham Estate a life-sized bronze statue of Persimmon, which was erected outside the stud at Home Farm.

* Jem Mace, born in Beeston, near East Dereham, in 1831, is regarded as the father of modern scientific boxing. He became world champion after beating Joe Goss in London in 1863. Mace defended his crown twice in America, retiring after the second bout when he drew over 12 rounds. He died in Liverpool but a white stone memorial was restored and moved to his home village in 1976. It stands outside the church where he was christened, son of the local blacksmith.

* Carrow Road is Norwich City Football Club's third home. The club, formed on Tuesday, June 17th, 1902, played at Newmarket Road in their earliest days. City made their debut in the professional field at Plymouth on September 2nd, 1905, losing 2–0.

They moved to The Nest for the start of the 1908–9 season. A disused chalkpit in Rosary Road was converted into a picturesque little stadium which was home until 1935.

* Norwich City beat West Ham 4–3 in front of a crowd of 29,779 when Carrow Road opened on August 31st, 1935. First goal on the new ground was scored by City skipper Doug Lochead. History was made at the ground on October 29th, 1938, when King George VI attended the City v Millwall fixture – the first time a reigning monarch had attended a Second Division match. City lost 2–0.

* When Norwich City supporters go all misty-eyed and talk of 'The Run' they are referring to the 1958–59 season when the Canaries reached the F.A. Cup semi-finals as a Third Division club. They lost 1–0 to Luton after a replay.

* Norwich City have won the League Cup twice. They beat Rochdale 4–0 on aggregate in 1962 when the final was a two-legged home and away affair. City's first Wembley success came in 1985 when they beat Sunderland 1–0 in what was then called the Milk Cup Final.

* With Ron Saunders as manager Norwich City first won promotion to Division One when they carried off the Second Division championship in 1971–72.

* Major Derek Allhusen of Claxton Manor, near Norwich, rode in the British team which won the gold medal in the three-day event at the Mexico Olympics in 1968. He won the individual silver medal on Lochinvar. In the Winter Olympics of 1948 he represented Great Britain in the pentathlon.

Norfolk proverb: The world gets better every day – then worse again in the evening.

Jimmy Bone (right) who scored Norwich City's first goal in Division One against Everton in August, 1972.

Fire and Flood

On Sunday, June 11th, 1615, while the inhabitants were in church, a fierce fire broke out in Wymondham. It resulted in 327 'persons and their families' losing property worth almost £14,000. The fire was started by gypsies and their fate is recorded in the parish register of St. Andrew's Church in Norwich under December 2nd, 1615: 'John Flodder and othere were executed for burning Windham.' They spelt the name of the town more sensibly in those days! With the formation of the Wymondham Volunteer Fire Brigade in 1882, the town was put on a sound fire-fighting footing.

* East Dereham has suffered two disastrous fires, the first in July, 1581, when nearly the whole town was destroyed. In October, 1679, 170 buildings were destroyed and five people lost their lives. It wasn't until 1862 that a public volunteer fire brigade was formed in Dereham. The most devastating blaze this century was in February, 1907, when fire destroyed Hobbies' engineering works, causing £25,000 worth of damage and putting 150 men out of work.

* A great fire destroyed much of Holt in 1708, and so the town is now mainly Georgian in appearance. At the north end, a ten-foot high milestone, erected after the fire, records distances to all the neighbouring villages and big houses.

* Watton was ravaged by fire on Saturday, April 25th, 1674, when over 60 houses and other properties were burnt down. The value of destroyed property was over £7000 and goods worth £2600 were also consumed. The town was given permission to collect all over England. There was such a good response to the appeal that rebuilding began quickly.

* Fire destroyed much of North Walsham in 1602. It claimed over 100 houses, 70 shops and warehouses, plus 500 barns, stables and other buildings. The Market Cross in the middle of the town was rebuilt after the fire.

* Fakenham's big blaze of 1738 saw the church 'thrice on fire'. About 40 houses were destroyed. Contemporary reports said the houses were lived in by the poorer people 'and therefore were of little consequence'.

* The lethal combination of an abnormally high tide and a vicious winter gale brought death and destruction to the Norfolk coast on the night of Saturday, January 31st, 1953. The death toll was 100 in Norfolk, while more than 300 people from Scotland to Kent lost their lives in the worst floods the east coast of Britain has seen. Over 5000 homes along the Norfolk coast were destroyed or badly damaged, and nearly 40,000 acres of farmland were flooded.

* The great flood of August, 1912, wreaked havoc in the county in general and in Norwich in particular, where at least two people died. Over seven inches of rain fell in about 12 hours, beating all previous figures for the British Isles, and matters were made worse by a north-westerly gale. Norwich Cathedral was threatened at one time, while thousands of people were washed out of their homes along the riverside.

* Norwich suffered severe flooding in November, 1878. There were boats in the streets and hundreds of people were made homeless. Three lives were lost. Even so, the highest recorded floods before the devastation of 1912 came in 1614.

* In Hunstanton's Esplanade Gardens there is a memorial plaque bearing the names of 31 people who lost their lives in the 1953 east coast floods, 15 of them British and the other 16 citizens of the United States. An American named Reis Leming saved 27 lives and was awarded the George Medal.

Tasty Morsels

Samphire, often known as poor man's asparagus, is a marsh plant that looks like seaweed and grows on the edge of tidal waters and marshes. Traditionally it was pickled to last through the winter after being gathered during July and August.

* The best cockles in Norfolk are said to come from Stiffkey, near Wells, and are known as Stewkey Blues because of their grey-blue shells.

* The herring made Great Yarmouth famous in the days when the eating of fish was compulsory on many days for religious reasons. It was salted and exported all over Europe. The Great Yarmouth Herring Fair, which lasted for 40 days, was first held in 1270 and continued well into the 18th century.

* Young swans used to be a local delicacy and could still be obtained up until the 1930s. In 1931 an advertisement appeared in the personal column of The Times for: 'Cygnets supplied dressed for dinners and banquets – Master, Great Hospital, Norwich'.

* Yarmouth produced the first mild smoke cure in 1835 and named the product a bloater. This is a whole, ungutted herring and is not split open down the back like a kipper. Natives of Yarmouth are still called 'Bloaters'.

* Cromer is famous for crabs. When you buy one at the fishmonger's it will have been boiled already. They are at their best from May to October. Cromer natives are called 'Crabs'.

* A number of varieties of apples originated in Norfolk, as their names tell us. Norfolk Coalman and Norfolk Dumpling were well known in the past, and you could also get Oxnead Pearmains and Horsham Russets. Mid-September was the usual time for starting the apple harvest, although superstitious pickers would wait until the 17th day after the appearance of the new moon in order to ensure sound fruit.

* Norfolk advice given to those wishing to cook a shellduck: 'Dew yew put a brick in the oven along with the bird. When the brick is sorft – so is the shellduck!'.

* The people of Norfolk are often known as 'dumplings' in honour of their favourite food as well as their solidarity and firmness. The true Norfolk dumpling is made with a bread dough containing yeast, or with a simple mixture of flour and water. It is known as a floater. Dumplings made of suet are known as sinkers or swimmers.

* Nothing was wasted in country households, and it was traditional to simmer a pig's head or extremities until very tender and then set the meat in its own jelly. The dish, known as brawn, dates from medieval times when it was served soused in a sharp vinegar sauce. In Norfolk the dish is known as pork cheese.

* Fairs were held in many towns and villages where people could enjoy a host of entertainments and buy little decorative ornaments and sweetmeats. Both the pieces of china and the biscuits and sweets were known as 'fairings', and the biscuits were known as Fair Buttons. They were either delicate and white or richly dark, flavoured with ginger. They were traditionally eaten at the Tombland Easter Fair in Norwich and at Yarmouth Easter Fair.

Norfolk at War

At 4.40 a.m. on July 10th, 1940, three Spitfires of No. 66 Squadron took off from Coltishall, the newly commissioned aerodrome eight miles north of Norwich, and climbed to 25,000 feet. Over Stalham they encountered a lone Dornier bomber. It was above them and as they climbed astern of it a German gunner raked one of the Spitfires with bullets and forced it to disengage. The other two pressed home their attack as the Dornier turned for home and eventually they shot it down in the sea. Only minutes later several German planes swooped down on Martlesham aerodrome, near Ipswich, and dropped 18 high explosive bombs along the edge of the airfield. This was the start of the Battle of Britain.

* A total of 677 aircraft crashed in Norfolk alone between the outbreak of hostilities and May 31st, 1945. The list included 92 Wellington bombers. Nearly 100,000 acres of Norfolk farmland were taken over by the USAF for airfields during the last war. In the last three years of the war when the 8th USAF was stationed in East Anglia, the best part of 6000 aircraft and 45,000 men were lost.

* The American Memorial Library, in the same building as Norwich Cathedral Library, was endowed and supported by the 2nd Air

Division USAF commemorating the 6300 Americans who lost their lives flying from Norfolk air bases in the last war.

* Film star James Stewart was stationed at Old Buckenham in the spring of 1944 as the 453rd Bombardment Group's executive officer. While he was there one of the group's squadrons, the 733rd, set an unbeaten record of 82 missions without loss.

* Air raids on Norwich from 1940 to 1943 claimed nearly 350 lives with over 1000 injuries. Over 2000 homes were destroyed and 2600 seriously damaged. The first raid on Norwich, on July 9th, 1940, killed 23 people. The heaviest raid came in late April, 1942. These were named 'Baedeker Raids' because Norwich appeared in Baedeker's 'British Isles' as a place of historic interest, and it was deliberately bombed for this reason. The two major assaults killed 231 citizens and injured nearly 700.

* The only church in the region destroyed in a wartime aircraft crash was that at Bawdeswell on November 6th, 1944. A Mosquito bomber from RAF Downham Market was returning from a raid when it crashed into All Saints' Church and burst into flames. Both crewmen were killed. A new church was built. A plaque commemorating the airmen and the tragic event was unveiled in November, 1990.

* The worst single air raid incident in Norfolk during the last war was at King's Lynn on June 12th, 1942. A lone Dornier dropped four bombs. Three caused little damage, but the fourth scored a direct hit on the Eagle Hotel where a 21st birthday party was being held. 42 people, 24 servicemen and 18 civilians, were killed and many others injured. The Eagle was rebuilt and opened again in September, 1959, the ceremony attended by two of the survivors of the 1942 bombing.

* Douglas Bader lost both legs in a fighter crash in 1931, but proved he could still fly on rejoining the RAF and playing a starring role in the Battle of Britain. He was given command of 242 Squadron at Coltishall, claiming ten Battle of Britain 'kills' and 13 others. He crashed in France in 1941, was captured and sent to Colditz Castle after escape attempts. He won the DSO, DFC, Legion d'Honneur and Croix de Guerre. His postwar work for the disabled won him a knighthood.

Odds and Ends

The Battle Area, in Breckland, where troops still train, was created during the last war by the evacuation of five villages – Stanford, Lynford, Tottington, West Tofts and Buckenham Tofts.

* The Midland and Great Northern Joint Railway was known as the 'Muddle and Get Nowhere' line. With a nostalgic sigh towards Melton Constable, once the Crewe of Norfolk, railway enthusiasts these days say it is 'Missed and Greatly Needed'. The line closed in 1959, although the Melton Constable to Sheringham line lingered on until 1964.

* The Prince of Wales, later King Edward VII, bought the Sandringham Estate in 1861. In 1870 a new house was built in the Jacobean style in brick with stone facings, and a second storey was added in 1891. Sandringham is popular with members of the Royal Family, especially for their winter stay.

* Lotus Cars, formed by Colin Chapman in London in 1955, moved to Hethel, near Norwich, in 1966. The former second world war airfield site saw the firm progress, selling cars to over 20 countries.

* Bernard Matthews, the Norfolk turkey tycoon who has made 'bootiful' a household word, bought a cheap incubator and 20 turkey eggs in 1950 – and so hatched the beginnings of a food empire which has transformed the modern poultry industry and eating habits.

* The Bishop of Norwich traditionally holds a service once a year in the ruins of St. Benet's Abbey at Ludham in Broadland. The service is held on the first Sunday in August, with the holiday season at its peak. The Benedictine monastery's beginnings go back to AD 816, and the last Abbot was made Bishop of Norwich. .

* The terminal at Bacton on the North Norfolk coast was built in 1967 to receive natural gas from the North Sea.

* After eight years of intensive trapping, the Norfolk campaign to wipe out the coypu was declared an official success in January, 1989. The South American rodent was introduced into East Anglia in 1929 for its pelt, the original population of 3000 expanding rapidly to an estimated 200,000 by the 1950s. The adult coypu, weighing about 20 lb and measuring two feet long, had a huge appetite for crops, including sugar beet and cereals.

* Arnold Wesker put Norfolk on the international stage with his play 'Roots'. It was first presented at the Belgrade Theatre in Coventry in May, 1959, with Joan Plowright taking the main role. Wesker worked and lived in Norfolk for some time and married a girl from Starston, near Harleston.

* Brickmaking in Costessey developed about 1800 to embellish Costessey Hall, and there were later two yards supplying the country at large. Barney brickworks, near Fakenham, continued in production until the 1960s.

* An airship station was built at Pulham St. Mary, near Harleston, during the First World War. The Air Ministry posted dirigible airships at Pulham, armed with machine guns and carrying bombs to attack German U-boats. They became known as 'Pulham Pigs' because of their shape. By the end of the war the Royal Navy had acquired a fleet of various airships, about 100 in all, and it was in 1919 that they came under RAF control.

* The R33 airship broke away from her moorings at Pulham on April 16th, 1925 – and hit the world headlines. There was a skeleton crew on board when the mooring arm snapped due to defective materials. A howling gale made normal handling difficult, and off she went a little after 8 a.m. Arrangements were made in Germany and Holland in case a forced landing was necessary after crossing the North Sea, but she managed to return to England. At Pulham the volunteers came out in force to get the ship down. The unscheduled flight had lasted 29 hours.

* The R101 disaster brought airship development in Britain to a halt, although the RAF station at Pulham had a role to play until closure came in 1957. The R101 crashed in Northern France on October 5th, 1930, on what was to have been her maiden flight to India. Of the 54 people on board only six survived the inferno. Many top men in the British airship industry, some of them with close Pulham links, died in the disaster.

E. DOW

Beeston echo – Miss Downs outside the village stores in mid-Norfolk.

* St. Faith's Fair was one of the most important fairs in East Anglia, lasting from the 15th century until 1872. It was held at Horsham St. Faith's near Norwich and tens of thousands of cattle changed hands, having been brought from north of the border by Scottish drovers.

* Reepham has the unique distinction of having three parish churches in the same churchyard, although All Saints has been a ruin since a fire in 1513. The other two still there are St. Mary's and St. Michael's.

* A mile east of Cawston, by the side of the B1149 and marked by a National Trust plaque, is the Duel Stone. It commemorates a duel between Henry Hobart of Blickling Hall and Oliver Le Neve of Great Witchingham Hall in 1698. Sir Henry died on the spot in the clash with his rival who had been elected Member of Parliament for Norwich in his place.

* The Pilgrim Fathers set sail from Plymouth for the New World in 1620. Of the 104 on The Mayflower, 76 were from East Anglia, including 32 from Norwich and Norfolk.

* Caister-on-Sea's lifeboat station was axed by the RNLI in 1969, but villagers, determined to keep their lifeboat history going, started an appeal to buy an independent boat. It was launched in 1972.

A Few Notables

Francis Blomefield (1705–1752) – Norfolk historian and Rector of Fersfield, near Diss, from 1729 until his death, printed his 'History of Norfolk' on his own press. He was working on the third volume when he was struck down by smallpox, and his history of the county was concluded by Charles Parkyn, Rector of Oxborough, near Swaffham.

* Howard Carter (1874–1939) – grew up in Swaffham and uncovered the treasures of the tomb of the Egyptian Tutankhamun in

1922. He had led the excavation work for ten years and it took him until 1933 to complete the removal of the crypt's objects.

* Edith Cavell (1865–1915) – the nurse from Norfolk shot by the Germans for helping Allied soldiers to escape during the First World War. She was born in Swardeston, near Norwich, where her father was vicar for nearly half-a-century. Nurse Edith Cavell's body was returned to her native county by popular demand and buried outside Norwich Cathedral.

* Dick Condon (1937–1991) – the Irish showman who turned Norwich's Theatre Royal into one of the most successful theatres in Europe after taking over as general manager in 1972. He also revived the defunct D'Oyly Carte company and ran summer seasons on the end of the pier in Cromer.

* Astley Cooper (1768–1841) – one of the leading surgeons of his time, Cooper was born at Brooke, near Norwich. He received a baronetcy for operating on George IV, who had a tumour in the scalp, and many other honours and successes followed.

* Bill Edrich (1916–1986) – a member of Norfolk's most famous cricketing family, he went on to represent Middlesex and England with distinction after cutting his teeth with Norfolk. He returned to captain his home county in 1959 and led them until 1968.

* George Edwards (1850–1933) – one of the key characters behind the formation of the National Union of Agricultural Workers, he was born at Marsham, near Aylsham, in abject poverty. At the age of 72 he was returned as Labour MP for the South Norfolk constituency. He is buried at Fakenham where an annual service of remembrance is held.

* Ted Ellis (1909–1986) – the Norfolk people's naturalist, he lived with his family for 40 years at Wheatfen Broad, Surlingham, in a remote cottage. A prolific writer and broadcaster, he was Keeper of Natural History at Norwich Castle Museum from 1928 until 1956. An honorary degree of Doctor of Science was conferred on this self-taught naturalist by the University of East Anglia in 1970.

* Elizabeth Fry (1780–1845) – was born at Earlham Hall, near

Norwich, and became a noted promoter of wide-ranging prison reforms both in England and on the Continent, particularly in the treatment of female prisoners.

* Henry Rider Haggard (1856–1925) – born at Bradenham, he wrote 50 books including the epic adventure 'King Solomon's Mines'. In later years he became a radical and reforming squire on returning to his native Norfolk, where he farmed at Ditchingham and Bedingfield.

* Robert Hales (1820–1863) – born at Somerton, near Great Yarmouth, he developed into the biggest man known in the western world at the time. He grew to 7ft.6in. and in his prime weighed 33 stone. He died of consumption and was buried in Somerton churchyard in a stone tomb.

* Sam Larner (1878–1965) – the Norfolk fisherman and traditional singer who was 'discovered' when he was nearly 80. With Harry Cox, the Winterton-born Larner represents the high point of East Anglian singing between the wars and immediately postwar.

* Arthur Patterson (1857–1935) – a self taught naturalist, who became an authority on Breydon Water, the estuary at Great Yarmouth which inspired much of his writing under the name of 'John Knowlittle'.

* Fuller Pilch (1804–1870) – the top batsman in England for over a decade, was born in Horningtoft, near Fakenham. He was lured away from the Norfolk cricket scene to Kent by an offer of £100 a year – and played until he was 51.

* Edward Seago (1910–1974) – one of the country's most popular landscape artists this century, was born in Norwich, the son of a coal merchant. He was a frequent visitor to Sandringham, and in 1956 accompanied Prince Philip on a trip to Antarctica. Seago was dogged by ill-health and died of a brain tumour at 53. His ashes were scattered over the Norfolk marshes he loved.

* George Skipper (1856–1948) – an architect famed for originality and sheer exuberance, he was born at East Dereham. Skipper made the Cromer skyline erupt with turrets and towers, and the exotic

extravagance of his hotels. He brought a touch of the Arabian Nights to the centre of Norwich with his Royal Arcade.

* Charles Townshend (1674–1738) – inherited the Raynham Estate and the title of second Viscount in 1687. He was a champion of progressive farming and earned the nickname of 'Turnip' Townshend from the root crop he introduced with such relish.

* James Woodforde (1740–1803) – whose diary, kept from the age of 18 until a few weeks before his death, is a mine of information about the lives of ordinary people in the second half of the 18th century. Parson Woodforde was appointed to the living of Weston Longville, a few miles from Norwich, in 1774.

> A Norfolk man wanted to be 'buried decent', and to this end he had his coffin made some years before it was likely to be needed. He kept it in the front room. During a serious illness, he was visited by the local parson. The old chap said, 'Dew yew go an' see that there corffin. Thass orl riddy.'
>
> The parson took a look and remarked to the man's wife what a handsome coffin it was. She replied, 'Yis, I spooz thass orryte, but I'll be glad to see the back onnit ... that dew clutter the plearce up so!'.

Little Dunham station.

TELL ME THE WAY

Tell me the Way

There are plenty of Norfolk place-names designed to give locals the chance to fall about in uncontrolled mirth as newcomers and visitors tumble headlong into the same old traps.

Of course, this practice is not peculiar to Norfolk, but it does seem to carry extra rations of relish in a county where the natives have been forced to put up with well-rehearsed jibes about being slow on the uptake but quick to reject all outside influences.

Can they be blamed for exacting some form of modest revenge in the shape of pronunciations and local corruptions which defy all logic? Little point in gatecrashing committee meetings being held in the darkest corner of The Rampant Ferret or The Eradicated Coypu unless you are conversant with local devious minds and tongues.

There may not be too much mileage left in Wymondham (pronounced Windham), Costessey (Cossey) or Happisburgh (Hazeburrer). But just watch faces light up when strangers ask the way to Alburgh, Guist, Hautbois, Postwick or Skeyton. 'Oh, you mean Arrburrer, not far from Harleston ... why dint yew say so in the first place?'.

There are also some mighty strange local abbreviations, Garboldisham is reduced to Garblesham and Hunworth to Hunny by more puckish members of the indigenous population. Beware the smiling folk who talk fondly of Hindol. They are referring to Hindolveston. And check very carefully before you seek directions to Ingoldisthorpe. This is another one melted down with the 'gold' extracted to leave Inglesthorpe.

Norfolk's delight in doing different gives Gillingham a hard 'G', unlike its much larger Kent counterpart. It remains a matter of considerable amazement – and amusement – that little Postwick, near Norwich, glories in really being Pozzick. Strangers have been known to shake their heads in disbelief when told Guist should come out as Guyst.

As you consult the following list of Norfolk place-names where the pronunciation is different from the spelling, bear in mind there may well be more than one local corruption or shortening. And as there are no firm rules when it comes to phonetics, there are bound to be a few arguments left unresolved. In many cases older residents are best judges of the 'proper' way to pronounce the name of the place where they live.

ACLE	*Aycull or Earcull (say quickly)*
ALBURGH	*Arburrer*
ALBY	*Orlby*
ASHMANHAUGH	*Ashmanorr*
AYLMERTON	*Elmerton*
AYLSHAM	*Elsham*
BARWICK	*Barrick (near Docking)*
BAWBURGH	*Borber*
BAWDESWELL	*Bordswell*
BEIGHTON	*Bayten*
BELAUGH	*Beloe or Beeler (near Wroxham)*
BLOFIELD	*Bloofield*
BURGH	*Burrer (near Aylsham)*
BURGH CASTLE	*Burrer Castle*
BERGH APTON	*Berrer Apton or Burg Apton (often made into one word)*
BYLAUGH	*Beloe or Beeler (near East Dereham)*
CALTHORPE	*Colthorpe (near Aylsham)*
CLEY	*Clay or Cly (support for both among locals, but mainly Cly)*
COLNEY	*Cooney*
COLTISHALL	*Coltshull*
COSTESSEY	*Cossey*
CROMER	*Croomer*
DEREHAM	*Deerum (East & West)*
DEOPHAM	*Deepham (some supporters for Deefum)*
DERSINGHAM	*Darsinum*
EARSHAM	*Errshum*
ELMHAM	*Ellam*
FAKENHAM	*Fakenum (first part to rhyme with bake) or Fearknum*

FIELD DALLING	*Field Dorlin' (often turned into one word)*
FLEGGBURGH	*Fleggburrer*
FORNCETT	*Fonsett*
FOULSHAM	*Foalshum*
FRANSHAM	*Franson (Little & Great)*
FULMODESTONE	*Fullmuston*
GARBOLDISHAM	*Garblesham*
GARVESTONE	*Garvestun or Garston*
GILLINGHAM	*with a hard 'G' (near Beccles)*
GUIST	*Guyst*
HAPPISBURGH	*Hazeburrer*
HARDINGHAM	*Hardnum*
HARGHAM	*Harfum (near Attleborough)*
HAUTBOIS	*Hobbis or Hobbies (Little & Great)*
HAVERINGLAND	*Haverland*
HELHOUGHTON	*Hellowton*
HEYDON	*Haydun*
HILGAY	*Hilgy*
HINDOLVESTON	*Hildosten or, more locally, Hindol*
HINDRINGHAM	*Hindrenum*
HOLME HALE	*Hoom Hale*
HOLME	*Hollem (the 'l' is sounded)*
HONING	*Hooning (don't confuse with Horning)*
HONINGHAM	*Hunningum*
HOVETON	*Hofton*
HUNSTANTON	*Hunstan*
HUNWORTH	*Hunny (a local delight to make it sticky for strangers!)*
INGOLDIS-THORPE	*Inglesthorpe*
ITTERINGHAM	*Ittrenhum*
KESWICK	*Kezzick*
LETHERING-SETT	*Larinsett*
LYNG	*Ling*
MATTISHALL	*Mattsull*
MAUTBY	*Morby*
MUNDESLEY	*Munnsley*

NARBOROUGH	...	*Narbrer*
NEATISHEAD	.....	*Neatsud*
NORTHREPPS	....	*Nordrupps (most colourful local corruption)*
NORWICH	....	*Norridge (to rhyme with porridge)*
OVINGTON	....	*Ovinton ('o' as in hover)*
PALLING	....	*Porlin'*
POSTWICK	....	*Pozzick*
PORINGLAND	.....	*Porland*
POTTER HEIGHAM	....	*Potter Hayam*
PUDDING NORTON	....	*Pudnorton (turned into one word)*
QUARLES	....	*Kworles (near Wells)*
RAVENINGHAM	..	*Raningham*
REEPHAM	....	*Reefum*
REYMERSTONE	..	*Remerstun*
ROUGHAM	....	*Ruffam*
ROUGHTON	....	*Rowton ('row' as in cow)*
RUNHALL	....	*Runnell*
RUSHALL	....	*Rewshull*
RYBURGH	....	*Ryburrer (Little & Great)*
SALHOUSE	....	*Sallus (don't confuse with Salthouse)*
SALLE	....	*Sorl*
SCOTTOW	....	*Scotter*
SCOULTON	....	*Scowton*
SHOTESHAM	....	*Shottsum*
SISLAND	....	*Sizzland*
SKEYTON	....	*Skytun*
SNETTISHAM	....	*Snettsum*
SOUTHREPPS	....	*Sudrupps (another colourful local version!)*
STANHOE	....	*Stanner*
STIFFKEY	....	*Stewkey (usually in association with 'Stewkey Blues' – Cockles)*
STODY	....	*Study*
SUTON	....	*Sewton (near Wymondham. Don't confuse with Sutton)*
SWAFIELD	....	*Swayfild*
SWAFFHAM	......	*Swoffum*

SWARDESTON	....	*Swordstun*
TACOLNESTON	...	*Tackleston*
TASBURGH	......	*Taysburrer or Tearsburrer*
TAVERHAM	......	*Tayverum or Tearverum*
THURSFORD	......	*Tharsfud*
THWAITE	....	*Twait*
TITTLESHALL	....	*Tittershull*
TIVETSHALL	.....	*Tivetsull*
TROWSE	....	*Troose (but open to debate!)*
WALCOTT	....	*Wolcutt*
WARHAM	....	*Worrum*
WALSHAM	....	*Wolshum (North & South)*
WATTON	....	*Wottun*
WEYBOURNE	.....	*Webbun*
WHEATACRE	.....	*Witteker (near Beccles)*
WHINBURGH	.....	*Winbrer*
WIVETON	....	*Wifton*
WOOD DALLING	..	*Woodorlin' (along same lines as Pudnorton)*
WORSTEAD	....	*Woosted*
WORTWELL	......	*Wurtell*
WRETHAM	....	*Rettum (East & West)*
WYMONDHAM	....	*Windum*
YARMOUTH	......	*Yarmuff*

There are many other potential pitfalls concerning places with similar-sounding names, as well as a batch of villages with the same name. Here are some useful tips on how to avoid confusion:

Bessingham is in North Norfolk – Bressingham is near Diss.
Booton is a small community near Reepham – Boughton is not far from Downham Market.
Bramerton is near Norwich – Brampton is three miles from Aylsham.
Brome is near Diss – Broome is near Bungay.
Dunston is on A140 just outside Norwich – Dunton is three miles west of Fakenham.
Gillingham is near Beccles – Gimingham is a few miles from Cromer.

Griston, with its prison, is close to Watton – Grimston is seven miles east of King's Lynn.
Hanworth is five miles north of Aylsham – Hunworth is two miles from Holt.
Ketteringham is six miles south-west of Norwich – Kettlestone is near Fakenham.
Langham is six miles from Holt – Longham is five miles from East Dereham.
Roxham is near Downham Market – Wroxham is at the heart of the Broads.
Salhouse is near Norwich – Salthouse is on the North Norfolk coast.
Suton is a couple of miles from Wymondham – Sutton is near Stalham.
Thornage is a few miles from Holt – Thornham is between Hunstanton and Brancaster

Don't muddle:
 Bacton, Wacton and Waxham.
 Snetterton and Snettisham.
 Caston, Coston and Cawston.
 Flitcham and Litcham.
 Brinton, Briston and Brisley.
 Eaton and Easton.
 Tittleshall, Tivetshall and Titchwell.
 Ringland and Ringstead.
 Reedham and Reepham.
 Rougham, Roughton and Roudham.
 Thurne, Thurning, Thurlton, Thurton and Thurgarton.
 Hoe and Howe.
 Honing and Horning.
 Oxnead, Oxwick and Oxborough.
 Stoke Ferry, Stoke Holy Cross and Stokesby.
 Hingham and Ingham (and note that self-effacing Lessingham is next door to Ingham)

There are several 'twins' living some way from each other. There is one Billingford near East Dereham and another near Diss. You can find one Croxton three miles east of Fakenham and the other three miles north of Thetford. Look out for a pair of Hardwicks, one near

King's Lynn and the other a few miles from Harleston. There's Roydon on the outskirts of Diss, and Roydon a few miles from King's Lynn.

Don't confuse the Wittons, one near Norwich and the other close to North Walsham. There's also Witton Green, near Reedham and Witton Bridge at Happisburgh. Norfolk has a couple of Hackfords, one with a Reepham flavour and the other close to Wymondham. Fritton near Yarmouth is a fair way from Fritton near Long Stratton.

Make sure you give the full name if you want to know the way to Oulton Broad near Lowestoft. You'll find Oulton on its own is a small community about three miles from Aylsham.

Newton's Lore is useful. Newton Flotman is seven miles south of Norwich. Newton St. Faith is four miles north of the city. There's little Newton next door to Castle Acre. West Newton is on the Sandringham Estate.

If you fancy a testing contribution to a Norfolk quiz on village names, just ask your eager panellists for the names of the only two villages with as few as three letters. Put them out of their misery with Hoe, near East Dereham, and Oby, not far from Yarmouth. The latter is also known as Ashby with Oby and used to be incorporated with Thurne as well in the West Flegg Hundred. White's Norfolk Directory of 1845 says 'Ashby with Oby and Thurne, at the north-western angle of West Flegg Hundred, were consolidated in one parish in 1604, and now comprise 262 inhabitants, of whom 177 are in Thurne, 69 in Oby and 16 in Ashby'.

Norfolk boasts four Beestons – Beeston Regis, near Sheringham: Beeston St. Andrew, near Norwich: Beeston St. Lawrence, near Wroxham and Beeston-with-Bittering, seven miles from East Dereham.

Make sure you know which Burnham you are after. Lord Nelson, Norfolk's most famous son, was born at Burnham Thorpe. There are six more close to each other – Burnham Market, Burnham Norton, Burnham Overy, Burnham Deepdale, Burnham Ulph and Burnham Westgate. In fact Burnham Overy is two villages, Overy Town and Overy Staithe ... so you can have the choice of eight.

The Thorpe business is flourishing, with Thorpe St. Andrew on the Norwich doorstep, much the largest of the family. Thorpe Abbots and Thorpe Parva are both near Diss; Thorpe Market is a few miles from Cromer; Thorpe Row is near East Dereham; Thorpe-next-Haddiscoe is five miles east of Loddon; Thorpe End, on the fringe of Norwich, runs into Great Plumstead; Thorpe Marriott is the newcomer demanding attention on the other side of the city.

While several 'partners' live closely together – like North and South Creake, Little and Great Cressingham, East and West Bradenham – there are several exceptions to the rule.

East Bilney is near Dereham while West Bilney is close to King's Lynn. North Walsham is an expanding town in North Norfolk; South Walsham is a village in Broadland. East Dereham is the town at the heart of Norfolk; West Dereham is a small settlement near Downham Market. (Matters have not been helped here by the decision of the bigger Dereham, deemed rather arrogant in some quarters, to dispense with the 'East' from its name).

There are other little twists. North Elmham is five miles from East Dereham (see how useful a full name can be!), while you have to go into Suffolk to find South Elmham. Little and Great Ellingham are neighbours near Attleborough – and there is an Ellingham going solo near Bungay.

Southwold goes its own genteel way on the Suffolk coast; Northwold is a long village a dozen miles from Thetford. Somerton and Winterton do rub shoulders not far from Yarmouth while it is a matter of regret to some that Norfolk does not yet boast a 'Springton' or 'Autumnton'.

Other points worth noting.... Don't confuse Barton Turf, near Wroxham, with Barton Bendish, between Swaffham and Downham. There's Belaugh near Wroxham, and Bylaugh near East Dereham. Both small parishes and both pronounced 'Beloe' or 'Beeler'.

You will find East and West Runton between Cromer and Sheringham. North and South Runcton and Runcton Holme are close to King's Lynn. East Ruston and Sco Ruston are a few miles from North Walsham. And don't mix any of those with East and West Rudham, a few miles from Fakenham.

Beware the Swanton connection. Swanton Abbott, Swanton Morley and Swanton Novers are nowhere near each other. Old and New Buckenham are close neighbours near Attleborough. Then there's

Buckenham Tofts near Thetford, and Buckenham on its own along the Norwich-Yarmouth railway line. It used to be known as Buckenham Ferry.

The Burgh family need careful inspection. Burgh on its own is near Aylsham, while Burgh Castle, Burgh St.Margaret and Burgh St. Peter are all close to Yarmouth. To add a bit more variety we have Burghapton, often spelt Bergh Apton, and they'll tell you it used to be billed as Burgh Apton in some old directories.

Don't muddle the Carleton clan – East Carleton, Carleton Forehoe, Carleton Rode and Carleton St. Peter (And there's Carlton Colville not far from Lowestoft).

Remember Cley is in North Norfolk while Cockley Cley is near Swaffham.

Eccles-on-Sea has an inland 'twin' near Attleborough.

Don't confuse Wood Dalling, Wood Norton, Field Dalling and Wood Rising. Then there's Woodbastwick, Woodton and the two Woottons near King's Lynn. Wolferton is where the trains used to stop for the Royal Family near Sandringham. Wolterton is near Aylsham.

Little and Great Plumstead are a few miles east of Norwich. Plumstead on its own is between Holt and Cromer.

Caister-on-Sea is next door to Yarmouth. Caistor St. Edmund is close to Norwich. Note they are spelt differently.

Don't mistake Holme Hale near Swaffham for for Holme-next-the Sea.

Houghton-on-the-hill is also near Swaffham, while Houghton St. Giles and Houghton of Robert Walpole fame are Fakenham way.
Martham is in the Fleggs near Yarmouth. Marham, with its RAF associations, is between Swaffham and Downham. Marsham, birthplace of Sir George Edwards, the farmworkers' leader, is near Aylsham.

The Meltons, Great and Little, are just beyond Norwich. Melton Constable, once at the hub of the local railway service, is six miles from Holt.

Saxlingham Nethergate is eight miles south of Norwich. Saxlingham is four miles from Holt.
Long Stratton and Stratton Strawless are well apart. So are Toft Monks, Toftrees and Toftwood.

Distinguish between Framingham Earl and Framingham Pigot,

and Horsham St. Faith and Newton St. Faith. And always remember a Norfolk village may have a 'shadow' just over the border or further afield. For example, there is a Brampton close to Aylsham and another one not far from Beccles. Bacton on the Norfolk coast has a 'twin' near Stowmarket.

They may sound very similar, but Aldborough is near Cromer, while Aldeburgh, with its wonderful music connections, is on the Suffolk coast.

Rhymes and jingles abound regarding Norfolk villages. Perhaps the most oft quoted is: Gimingham, Trimingham, Knapton and Trunch, Northrepps, Southrepps, all in a bunch.

Another popular way of demonstrating the Norfolk capacity for self mockery is found in little gems like: 'It's called 'Silly Sutton' because the locals used to thrust their hands through the open windows to see if it was daylight!'

A more flattering line for another village: 'Blessed are they that live near Potter Heigham – and double blessed are they that live in it!' Perhaps that owes something to having Sidney Grapes, the Norfolk comedian, as a resident all his life.

Everyone in Norfolk should know the last place to be named in the county. Records do not show if it was Great or Little when The Blessed Name-giver looked at his list and sighed after over seven hundred little ceremonies: 'That's Dunham!'

An old Norfolk countryman who had lived in the same parish for over 80 years was approached by a newcomer.

'There's a funny lot of people living in this district' said the newcomer.

'Ah' replied the old countryman, 'An thass a funny thing, they dew keep a' cummin' here anorl!'.

Dereham Road, Litcham.

WHAT THEY SAY

What They Say

If it is nigh impossible to see ourselves as others see us, we still like to know all the latest gossip. The fact that they are talking about us, either from afar or over the garden wall, remains one of Norfolk's strangest delights.

We love to snarl when the national media haul out the 'Sleepy East Anglia' stickers as soon as the likes of Norwich City or Ipswich Town cock a snook at soccer's traditional fortresses. We react fairly smartly to stereotype fun and games. That's remarkable in itself for a straw-chewing, dour and unimaginative lot with three speeds – slow, dead slow and backwards.

Generalisations can be dangerous as well as dismissive, but we've had to put up with them for centuries. Perhaps they have helped stiffen the backbone.

Charles II claimed Norfolk was fit only to be cut up for roads for the rest of the country. Horace Walpole pointed to the 'wilds of Norfolk' as districts to be shunned rather than sought out. Noel Coward didn't take long to sum the place up. 'Very flat, Norfolk' said one of the Master's voices, probably after a short yodel in the Himalayas.

Had he taken the trouble to ask, we could have told him there is as much variety here as in any scene from 'Private Lives'. In altitude, the county ranges from three feet below sea level in Stow Bardolph Fen to 340 feet on the coastal ridge at West Runton. One can savour numerous and ever-changing views across short distances. What about Norfolk skies? The vast difference between, say, Breckland and Broadland?

Of course, a few unruly characters have tried to give the place a bad name over the years. John Wesley, the founder of Methodism, described Norfolk people as contentious and quarrelsome, especially in Norwich.

Preaching at the Tabernacle in 1759 he found a 'large, rude and noisy congregation', and Wesley was moved to tell them they were the most ignorant, conceited, self-willed, fickle, intractable, disorderly, disjointed society in the three kingdoms. I don't know what the collection amounted to on that occasion – or even if he decided to take one – but there can be little doubt that standards had improved by the time American evangelist Billy Graham headed this way just over two centuries later.

Wesley paid his first visit to Great Yarmouth in 1761. He wrote of the place in his journal: *'A large and populous town, and an eminence for wickedness and ignorance as any seaport in England.'* However, King's Lynn made a good impression on the great travelling preacher when he went there for the first time ten years on. He found the people affable and humane, open and frank, good-natured and courteous. Perhaps the fact they gave him a respectful hearing influenced him in this glowing estimate.

Dr. Augustus Jessopp, writing in 1890 as the Rector of Scarning, near East Dereham, delivered these memorable lines: *'Always shrewd, the Norfolk peasant is never tender; a wrong, real or imagined, rankles with him through a lifetime.... Refinement of feeling he is quite incapable of.'*

At least Jessopp was reasonably close to the folk he felt obliged to take to task. All too often in more recent times Norfolk has had to endure cheap and nasty jibes from smart metropolitans firing away from a safe distance. A notorious attack was featured in the Arts pages of The Sunday Telegraph in July 1991.

Prolific writer A. N. Wilson, a Fellow of the Royal Society of Literature, turned his talents to sizing up the week's television programmes under the headline of 'Mad but normal for Norfolk'. Out of his disappointment in a play with a rural setting he contrived this savage summary:

'I know of a medical practice in rural East Anglia where the majority of the patients are inbred, hare-lipped, mental defectives. When they put their boot faces round the surgery door and pour out their tales of woe to the doctor, the GP writes 'N.F.N.' on their notes. It means 'Normal For Norfolk'.

'As well as being very flat, Norfolk is full of curmudgeonly human monsters. Tucked away in their bleak villages beneath the large threatening sky, they are still as belligerent as they were in the days of Queen Boadicea.'

I wonder why?

A. N. Wilson (Rugby, New College, Oxford), born in Staffordshire and raised in Wales, then decided this 'miserable play' had real value after all. It had served as *'a useful antidote for anyone watching it who might be tempted, as yuppies in the 1980s used to be, by the idea of a second home in some Norfolk village where property, like human life, is cheap.'*.

A mixture of anger and pity gave way to grudging gratitude for making would-be settlers think carefully before throwing in their lot with belligerent peasants in bleak villages under a threatening sky.

A month later, some measure of mercy had to be afforded Anti-Norfolk Wilson as The Sunday Times, in a special investigation in their Style and Travel section, featured him as a fully paid-up member of The Snobbocracy, a journalistic elite lording it at The Spectator and Sunday Telegraph.

Mr. Wilson, declared this special investigation, wrote in the tone of Lady Bracknell, though without her humour. He was labelled an Absolute Snob – and there were few notes of protest from Norfolk.

I don't know of any specific reasons for Mr. Wilson's vitriolic outburst – and he did not reply to my curt but polite letter of inquiry on the subject – but the need to sell newspapers, even in the so-called 'quality' arena, should not excuse such grubby blanket condemnation of an entire county.

Norfolk has put up with plenty of good-natured ribbing about being on the road to nowhere and trying to keep the old drawbridge intact ... indeed, one suspects many of the 'backwater' comments have been born out of envy. Even those in the vanguard of The Development Express roaring through the county in the past decade or so must have caught at least a fleeting glimpse of what was being replaced.

There's also an element of admiration in back-handers like: 'The only way to lead Norfolk people is first to find out which way they are going – and then march in front of them'. It's one thing to be noticed for being different, and to be amiably chastised for it, but most Norfolk stalwarts draw the line at being asked to apologise for following natural instincts.

H. J. Harcourt, writing in the Norfolk Magazine in 1948, summed it up thus:

'Strangers who come into our midst are inclined to treat us either with benevolent condescension or with undisguised supercilliousness – and then expect us to acclaim them as saviours and the harbingers of civilisation.'

Bernard Dorman, in the introduction to his book on the county first published in 1972, said: *'The wisdom of long experience in the art of living does not take kindly to enthusiasts who would make sweeping changes. It wears them down so that in the end it is the innovators who are changed.'*

Doreen Wallace, who compiled the Norfolk volume in the County Books series with Dick Bagnall-Oakeley in 1951, underlined the dangers of making too many generalisations before putting the native-newcomer debate into perspective:

'It is a fact that after a "foreigner" has lived 20 years in the county, he is still a new arrival; he may, however, be accepted by that time as the kind of new arrival who will be made welcome if he cares to settle down.'

Not an ounce of charity in sight, however, in another of those infuriatingly-broad surveys designed to raise Norfolk blood pressures and a posh magazine's circulation at the end of October in 1992.

The county was branded the most unfriendly in the United Kingdom, along with Yorkshire, with Mileham singled out for the title of worst village in the country for accepting newcomers. The survey conducted by Country Life magazine considered only a sample of parishes across the United Kingdom, and the researcher admitted she had not spoken to any Suffolk or Cambridgeshire residents. Nor was it made clear how the whole business had been conducted among Norfolk natives or newcomers. After all, it is important what you ask, how you ask it and who is invited to give answers.

'Norfolk is still very rural and determined not to let commuters in unless they absolutely have to,' said Country Life. The same old story of confusing caution with coldness and pride with prejudice, although the magazine did have the grace to suggest Norfolk was more likely to accept newcomers if they took an active part in village life. A reasonable sort of rule to apply, anywhere.....

Norfolk County Council chief executive Barry Capon, whose career brought him to the county from his native Sussex 21 years before, dismissed the survey as 'absolute twaddle', and posed the obvious question:

'If it were so awful then why do so many people move here and stay here?'

Some of those people stepped forward smartly to join the rush to write letters to the Eastern Daily Press. They were prepared to meet the natives halfway along the road to peaceful co-existence in Norfolk in general and in much-maligned Mileham in particular.

There'll be more of these sweeping generalisations – you know, it takes 25 years to be accepted in this village and they still stick pins into effigies of non-native stock in that one – but Norfolk must continue to play a straight bat on the stickiest of wickets.

Mind you, some contributions can bring a fresh and valuable perspective to the Norfolk picture. I was particularly impressed by an article in The Wall Street Journal in March, 1993, and not just because their reporter Tony Horwitz based much of it in my home village of Beeston, seven miles from East Dereham.

The Ploughshare pub had closed a few months before.... *'Beeston was suddenly like hundreds of other villages across Britain – without a social hub. The passing of village pubs reflects, as well as hastens, the demise of traditional village life. In Beeston, as elsewhere, the village school, church and store are at risk as the population ages and newcomers commute for work, shopping and entertainment.'*

Our American correspondent drew telling comparisons between the self-sufficiency running through much of Norfolk village life a century ago and the fear of becoming just another pretty dormitory so prevalent today. He examined the gulf between locals and newcomers. On the one hand, newcomers didn't like *'the smell of manure and the sound of tractors'*. On the other, according to a Londoner who had worked at the Ploughshare and other rural pubs, *'These villages have a Hitchcock quality, full of dark looks and old feuds. You have to set your watch back 200 years'*.

Obvious exaggerations, but offered as handy antidotes to any lingering insistence on seeing our villages as a quaint paradise of rose-covered cottages and chiming cowbells.

The Wall Street Journal prompted a far more vigorous and healthy exercise in self-examination that month than The Tatler.

The magazine spattered with hyphens, titles and hyperbole took the lid off the *'East Midlands Mafia'*, a smart set who find anywhere from Hunstanton to Blakeney – with the exception of Wells (*'full of naff souvenir shops and teeming with caravans'*) – socially acceptable.

We were treated to little gems like: *'The Norfolk scene is rather like stepping into Arthur Ransome's Swallows and Amazons'* and *'The very pretty Georgian market town of Burnham Market is the Sloane Street of the coast'*. When the article referred to the local paper as the Eastern Daily Express I realised we must not take this sort of thing too seriously.

The way Norfolk people speak has long been a source of mystery and amusement to the rest of the civilised world. The fact that the vast majority of television and radio productions with a Norfolk setting have to be satisfied with *'Mummerzet'* accents will continue to anger the indigenous population and annoy all those who care about accuracy. After all, strenuous efforts are made to get other accents right and it seems a tame excuse to complain that the Norfolk vernacular is so hard to imitate.

Dick Bagnall-Oakeley, dialect expert, naturalist and geography teacher at Gresham's School in Holt, claimed he was bilingual – and proved it with many memorable renditions in both orthodox English and the local tongue. He provided this telling summary in 1974: *'Norfolk is not simply a word that describes a county. "Norfolk" describes also a language, a humour and a way of life. Spoken Norfolk has a stout and uniquely resistant quality and only people born in the county are able properly to penetrate it and repeat it with their own tongues.*

'Just as their language, so also the people of Norfolk are tough, resistant and impenetrable. They guard to themselves the secrets of their language and of their humour. Yet humour there is in the Norfolk people, riotous and abundant. When you read Norfolk tales, remember that they are tales about a highly observant, subtle and recondite people. Therefore, always think twice before you laugh at a Norfolk tale – the laugh might be on you!'.

Doreen Wallace looked closely at the old criticism of people in these here parts being a bit slow on the uptake:

'Any political candidate who has addressed a Norfolk meeting will

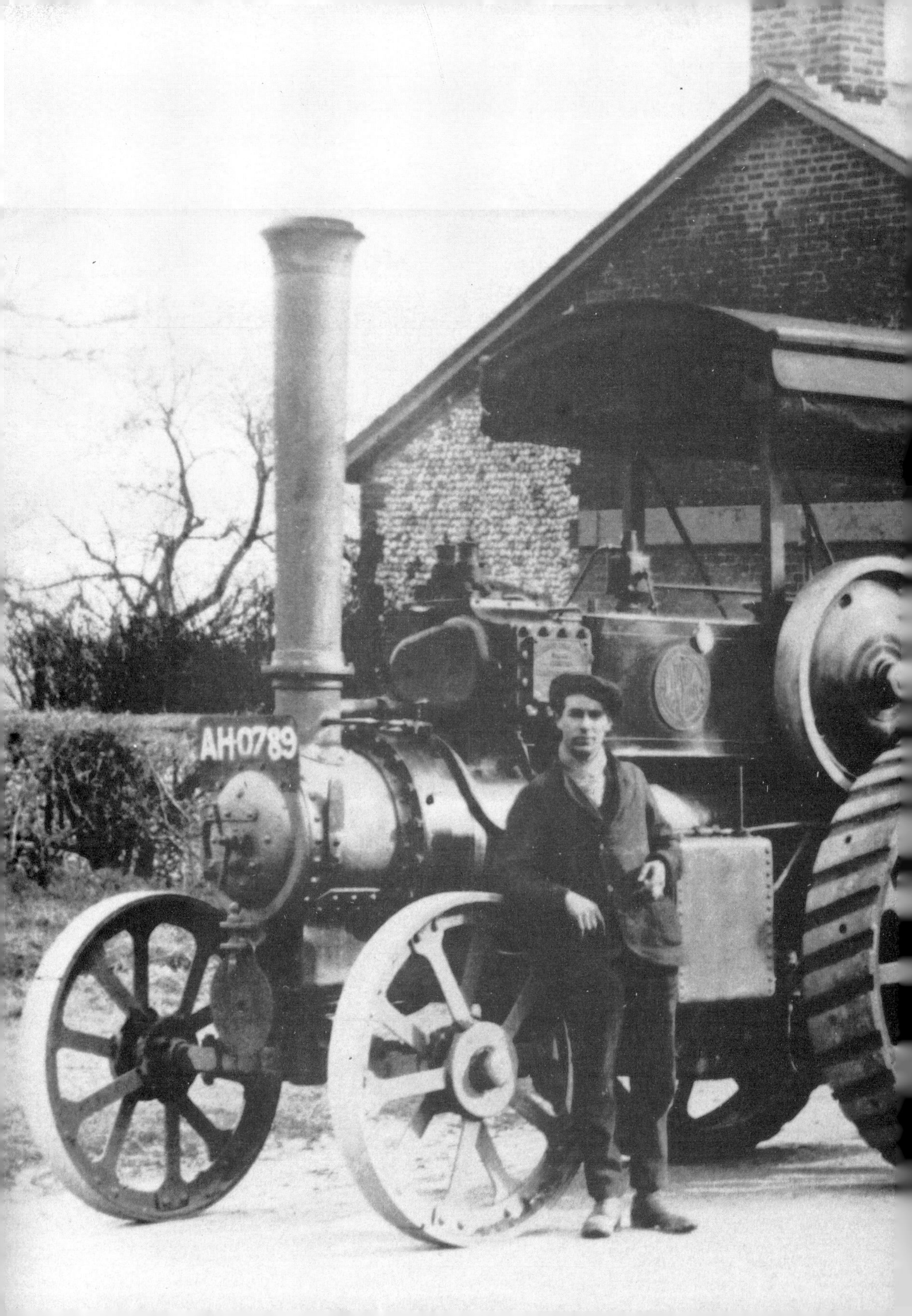
AH 0789

Getting up steam at Beetley.

agree with me, I think, that the audience is slow to laugh, slower still in its reaction to pathos or indignation, and slowest of all in applause. But it may be this isolationist pride of them, and not stupidity at all.... Norfolk people are at least sincere; they wear their demerits on the outside and their virtues within, so you are seldom taken in by them.'

There remain many in the county anxious to refute suggestions that lack of speed is a blatant sign of weakness...be it on the hustings or on Norfolk's much-criticised roads.

William Cobbett took in these parts in 1821 during his epic 'Rural Rides'. He had a little go about the flatness – something to laud, I would have thought, for a traveller on horseback – but softened the blow with a eulogy that ought to be pinned on the visitors' dressing-room door at Carrow Road, in every seaside guest-house and on the podium in Brussels:

'The Norfolk people are quick and smart in their motions and in their speaking. Very neat and trim in all their farming concerns, and very skillful. Great admiration for this county of excellent farmers and hearty, open and spirited men.'

While we are ploughing the fields and scattering sound words on the land, let's recall a visit to Norfolk by A. G. Street from his Wiltshire home in the early 1930s. The countryman-writer was soon told how to sort out the wheat from the chaff:

'From the conversation at the dinner table on the first evening, I gather that my great crime against Norfolk is that I, a mere Southerner, have dared to criticise the county in any way whatsoever. Apparently, Norfolk is beyond criticism ... and my hosts did their best to show me the error of my ways.

'Norfolk's farming community does not approve of interlopers from other parts of Great Britain, and especially when these aliens make a success of their farming. One has to be born and bred in Norfolk to fit in properly. ... But what a lovely unspoilt land Norfolk is! Modern civilisation, with its hustle and bustle and noise, seems to have passed it by'

Mr. Street looking for the right road. J. B. Priestley, who embarked on his famous 'English Journey' in the autumn of 1933, was not too hard pushed to pen a song of praise as he sized up Norfolk and its people:

'A solid man. Lots of beef and beer, tempered with the east wind, have gone to the making of him. Once he is sure you are not going to cheat him or be very grand and affected he is a friendly chap; but if you want the other thing you can have it. Perhaps we of the West Riding brought some of our aggressive qualities from Norfolk.'

On his way to becoming Vicar of East Dereham in 1850, the Rev. Benjamin Armstrong found this pat on the back in an inn:

'Evidently from the pen of a Norfolk man, but from general report it is not very far from the truth....'Whether we survey the county with regard to the climate, population, commerce, the character of the inhabitants, its diversified beauties, or the improved state of its agriculture, it may with propriety be termed the glory of England.'

Similar sentiments from Sir Thomas Browne in the 17th century.... *'Let any stranger find me out so pleasant a county, such good ways, large heaths, three such places as Norwich, Yarmouth and Lynn in any county in England, and I'll be once again a vagabond and visit them.'*

More of the same in 1940 from Arthur Mee in his book on Norfolk in 'The King's England' series.... *'For the traveller in search of the English heritage, this county is a paradise. It has great cliffs and chalk downs, a history far older than any written documents, delightful rivers, unique still waters, low-lying fens, captivating towns, a historic roll of famous folk and a group of Saxon, Norman and medieval churches crammed with the beauty that makes England the matchless country of the world.'*

There are many other examples, some less flattering than others. However, the majority underline the strength of the Norfolk character, the qualities of the landscape in which it has been fashioned and the rewards waiting for those prepared to explore them. Virginia Gay, who was born in Ghana and studied history at the University of East Anglia, had settled in Norfolk by the time she produced her first novel, 'Penelope and Adelina', first published by Sinclair-Stevenson in February,1992. A dual narrative left plenty of scope for references to the county she had grown to love as the story came up to date....

'The journey into Norfolk is famously difficult. It's kept that way pour decourager les autres. Things have not changed much since Parson Woodforde's time. Tea on the train is horrible swill. If they

feel so inclined the drivers bring the trains to a clanking halt at Shenfield or perhaps just outside Diss. If you complain too bitterly then they will tell you that somebody has thrown himself under the wheels of the train and that they are waiting to clear the body and scrub the track. It's all done in order to make you feel ashamed, to oblige you to bear up and take it like a man. They especially like to remind you that you have not paid for your seat at all, but only for the privilege of travelling on one of their trains. The A11, too, is a monstrously inconvenient road, dangerous as well. There's a mist that comes down like the clappers in the hollows of Thetford Forest. People quickly get bored of waiting behind lorries full of sugar beet, not to mention lumbering tractors. They overtake when they can't see a thing.

'Just the same, the sight of your first pink-washed farmhouse is worth all the trouble....'

Sentiments backed by countless visitors and settlers in recent years. You can almost hear the old Norfolk die-hard muttering about customs and passports and the need to rediscover that brand of hostility so rife in the days of Boadicea.

In picking some more plums from my collection I hope to illustrate why this old county with its backside sticking into the North Sea has been known to display a belligerent streak. The selection also underlines the wealth of rich literature Norfolk has inspired. Many of the volumes to which I refer have long been out of print, but a search along the shelves of any local second-hand book shop should bring worthwhile prizes.

Norfolk Nuggets

If the rest of Britain sank beneath the waves, and Norfolk was left alone, islanded in the turmoil of the seas, it would, I think, survive without too much trouble ... Norfolk has always stood alone and aloof from the rest of England. – James Wentworth Day. 1976, (Norwich Through the Ages).

Why go to the Alps or hanker after the Mediterranean, or think of Germany – pshaw! – when a sort of Eden by the Yare winds round the bends. – *Arthur Patterson, 1920 (Through Broadland In A Breydon Punt)*.

Although Norfolk is one of the driest counties in England because of its extreme eastern position, still it does have rain, and when it is in earnest, it does come down, too. – *Ernest Suffling, 1899 (How To Organise A Cruise On The Broads)*.

The little town of Watton left behind, we soon entered upon a wild wooded country where the signs of human habitation were few and far between. – *James John Hissey, 1889, (A Tour in a Phaeton)* NB Phaeton = a light open carriage drawn by two horses.

New beauties are perceptible with each succeeding dawn – a tinge of green here, a richer purple there, sun and cloud weaving the warp and woof of the panorama of colour in the landscape, flashing on the silver trunk of a birch or the ruddy richness of a Scots pine or plunging the distant woodland into a haze of blue. – *W. G. Clarke, 1923 (In Breckland Wilds)*.

I can remember walking through this sparcely populated district on my way to Happisburgh late in the afternoon of a day in early spring. All day the fresh furrows of the hedgerow fields had been white with seagulls, for near the coast more gulls than rooks or grey crows follow the plough. – *William Dutt, 1909. (The Norfolk and Suffolk Coast)*.

> *On the grass of the cliff, at the edge of the steep,*
> *God planted a garden – the garden of sleep!*
> *'Neath the blue of the sky, in the green of the corn,*
> *It is there that the regal red poppies are born!*
– *Clement Scott 1886 (The Garden Of Sleep: A Summer Song)*.

The first time I ever gorged myself with Yarmouth rock on Yarmouth beach the ancient monuments in which I was most interested were the bathing machines. Out of these came dozens of the fattest women I have ever seen, in frilly bathing costumes that came down to their knees. – *Eric Fowler, 1947 (Jonathan Mardle – 'As I Was A'Sayin'')*.

A fine old city, truly, is that, view it from whatever side you will; but it shows best from the east, where the ground, bold and elevated, overlooks the fair and fertile valley in which it stands. – *George Borrow 1851 (writing about Norwich in 'Lavengro').*

You can see the past effect of ownerships and individuality in Lynn as clearly as you can catch affection or menace in a human voice. The outward expression is most manifest, and to pass in and out along the lines in front of the old houses inspires in one precisely those emotions which are aroused by the human crowd. – *Hilaire Belloc, 1906 (The Hills And The Sea).*

> *When erst in youth's gay prime and uncontrolled*
> *O Thetford! round the flow'ry fields I've strolled,*
> *From Tutt-Hill's eminence and Croxton's height,*
> *Have viewed thine ancient ruins with delight.*
> *– George Bloomfield, 1821, (Thetford Chalybeate-Spa).*

Norfolk would not be Norfolk without a church tower on the horizon or round a corner up the lane. We cannot spare a single Norfolk church. When a church has been pulled down the country seems empty or is like a necklace with a jewel missing. – *John Betjeman, 1972 (Norfolk Country Churches And The Future).*

The first sight of Blickling Hall is one of the greatest surprises that can possibly befall the traveller in search of the picturesque. – *Charles Harper, 1904 (The Newmarket, Bury, Thetford and Cromer Road).*

I have had another opportunity of visiting Holkham; I have again been gratified in seeing one of the finest places in the kingdom, whose scenery, combining the different picturesque beauties of rich, varied and highly decorated ground of magnificent wood, expanded water, and extended projects, including occasional views of the sea, cannot but delight every lover of nature, and more than meet the high raised expectations of the admiring stranger. – *Edward Rigby. 1819 (Holkham, its agriculture – in 'The Pamphleteer').*

Of the park we have to speak in high terms. Like the true English park of the better caste, it forms a magnificent piece of human skill and industry, yet exhibiting no mark of either, and, to the uninitiated, reposing in the same natural outline it had at the beginning. It looks like Nature's own production. – *James Grigor, 1841 (writing about Felbrigg in 'The Eastern Arboretum').*

The great piece of husbandry in which Norfolk excels is in the management of turnips, from which it derives an inestimable advantage. – *Nathaniel Kent, 1796 (General View of Agriculture In The County Of Norfolk).*

Some enchantment lies upon the coast of North Norfolk which leaves it in memory, not just an impression of peculiar beauty, but a series of pictures standing out as vividly as if you had opened a book. – *Lilias Rider Haggard, 1946 (A Norfolk Notebook).*

It was the least changed part of old England, with only a few visitors in summer. This was attractive to me after the Devon coast, which had changed so rapidly since I had known it, becoming built upon, and populous. – *Henry Williamson, 1941 (The Story Of A Norfolk Farm).*

In 1856 I entered upon my first harvest ... When the wheat was carted I led the horse and shouted to the loaders to hold tight when the horse moved. When this work was finished and there was nothing further for me to do, I went gleaning with my mother. – *George Edwards, 1922 (From Crow-Scaring To Westminster).*

I was quite tired, and very glad when we saw Yarmouth. It looked rather spongy and soppy, I thought, as I carried my eye over the great dull waste that lay across the river; and I could not help wondering if the world were really as round as my geography book said, how any part of it came to be so flat. – *Charles Dickens, 1849 (David Copperfield).*

We listened to other boomings as we were quanted home, and as we stepped out on the lodge lawn in the falling dark of the June evening there came across the water the calls that I had never thought to hear together – a bittern's and a cuckoo's. – *Eric Parker, 1929 (English Wild Life).*

So great was the change from the bustle of fashion to this unbroken quiet that I could scarcely believe that I was only parted by a dip of coastline from music and laughter and seaside merriment, from bands and bathing machines, from crochet and circulating libraries. – *Clement Scott, 1886 (Poppyland Papers)*.

The North Sea here is as dark as anywhere in Britain, and the locals still often refer to it by its stark ancient name, the German Ocean. – *Richard Mabey, 1987. (A Tide In The Affairs)*.

Yarmouth, the paradise of excursionists ... one scarcely knows how to take it, so to say, whether to look upon it as the haunt pure and simple of the cheap 'tripper' or to regard it as a quaint old seaport, picturesque in the highest degree, interesting from end to end; a place wherein to study the old 'salt' in his native lair, or to take 'impressions' of the East-end holidaymaker in his most festive mood. – *Annie Berlyn, 1894 (Sunrise-Land . . . Rambles In Eastern England)*.

Never be ashamed of the dialect and customs of good old Norfolk. If we are behind the times compared with other counties, we can console ourselves with the thought that Norfolk men have played their part, and that right well, in the stirring events of our nation's history. – *Walton N. Dew, 1896 (A Dyshe Of Norfolke Dumplings)*.

Norfolk is still one of the most beautiful counties in England and has probably been able to hang on to its real character longer than most because of its geographical position. When I talk to people who have known the county more years than I can remember they tell me that I have already missed the best, that times have changed very much since the war and the atmosphere of the place is not anything like as quiet as it used to be. – *Edward Storey, 1978 (Call It A Summer Country)*.

'Rare and beautiful Norfolk' as John Sell Cotman called it in 1841, is undoubtedly less rare and beautiful than it was, but we have some grounds for hope. In the first place an increasing number of people care about the county, its buildings and its landscapes. – *David Dymond, 1985. (The Norfolk Landscape)*.

There is no better playground in England, and certainly none easier of access or more cheaply to be enjoyed. – *George Christopher Davies, 1883 (Norfolk Broads And Rivers)*.

Since the war the popularity of sailing has brought about a massive increase in boat ownership and boating holidays all round the county, and on the Broads the traffic has increased to such an extent that the quiet waterways out of season have, during the long holiday months, become almost as busy as the roads. – *Geoffrey Morgan, 1991 (East Anglia – Its Tideways And Byways)*.

All England may be carved out of Norfolk, represented therein not only to the kind but degree itself. Here are fens and heaths, and light and deep, and sand and clay ground, and meadows and pastures, and arable and woody, and (generally) woodless land; so grateful is this shire with the variety thereof. Thus, as in many men, through perchance this or that part may justly be cavilled at, yet all put together complete a proper person; so Norfolk, collectively taken, hath a sufficient result of pleasure and profit, that being supplied in one part which is defective in another. – *Thomas Fuller, 1662 (Worthies Of England)*.

The trouble with many of us native residents of the place is that we are so often thinking how much more beautiful Norwich was in the past or might yet be in the future if only we looked after it properly, that it is not easy for us to evaluate it as it is now. We discredit our own achievements, and those of all our ancestors as far back as our great-great-grandfathers. There is an antiquarian snobbery about it which forbids us to admit comeliness for anything built since the Regency. – *Eric Fowler, 1950 (Jonathan Mardle on The Beauties of Norwich in the Eastern Daily Press)*.

On the whole, despite their annual summer invasion, Norwich and the Broads remain supremely beautiful, coolly conscious of the space and dignity of ancient buildings, of wide green marshes, shining waters and noble sky-scapes which make the Broadland picture. Whether the threatened creation of a National Park will enhance or improve the scene is, to my mind, doubtful. I do not believe in the dead hand of remote bureaucratic control. Those who dwell in and by the English countryside are the best guardians thereof. – *James Wentworth Day, 1953 (Norwich And The Broads)*.

Despite enormous commercial pressures, there is still magic here; there are still places where a soul can escape, where water-lilies flourish and dragonflies dip over clean water dykes. – *David Dane, 1989. (David Dane's Broadland)*.

This afternoon we made our way through the green lanes of primrose country to the Bath Hills of Ditchingham, there to be bewitched by the gentle Waveney, the far-rimmed plain of Cutney Common and the strange steep slopes of tree-clad inland cliffs. We had the feeling we had invaded a secret paradise, a lost valley, a rare new Norfolk, so lovely and so enfolding the life and sunlight within it that it seemed almost unreal. – *Ted Ellis, 1953. (Secret Paradise, Eastern Daily Press)*.

The only trouble about motoring through Norfolk is that however slowly you go (and even in Norfolk other drivers get impatient if you hesitate) marvels flash by you. – *Paul Jennings, 1986 (East Anglia – watercolours by John Tookey, Words by Paul Jennings)*.

Better the evils that we know. I was much amused at a Women's Institute meeting to see over forty women vote solidly against living in a town (after a very able debate on advantages of town and country), leaving the proposer and supporter for the town in solitary glory. In spite of the fact that country women can be very vocal upon their grievances, I fancy they know well enough which is the fuller life for them. – *Lilias Rider Haggard, 1936 (Norfolk Life)*.

It is a privilege to be able to stroll through these lanes or on the saltmarshes or along the river valleys, with the quietness all round and that huge open sky above. Even in the winter when the fields are bleak and the wind is bitter, somehow the world seems a gentler, a calmer, a more civilised place. – *John Timpson, 1990. (Timpson's Travels In East Anglia)*.

Of later years many interesting birds and animals once plentiful in Norfolk have become either rare or extinct. This is owing partly to the better drainage of the marshes, the introduction of better guns and, in later years, to the invasion of a host of cockney visitors. – *H. E. H. Gillett, 1898 (Bygone Norfolk)*.

If our authentic East Anglian rural scenery – our common heritage – is lost, not only will those who love beauty as a sure escape from the ugliness of life suffer, but the whole vast network of business interests who cater, directly or indirectly, for summer visitors and tourist traffic will slowly but surely reap the unpleasant reward of their indifference. – *Lilias Rider Haggard, 1943 (Norfolk Life)*.

The small farmer, unable to afford the fashionable large machines, is often persuaded to sell up, and more and more land is coming under the ownership of business-men and corporations, who see the countryside simply in terms of an investment. – *David Yaxley, 1977 (Portrait of Norfolk)*.

The inhabitants of Breckland sustain the impression created by their surroundings. They often complain that they have been invaded, that they are living under conditions which would scarcely be any different were an enemy army in occupation. American and British troops have taken possession of huge areas of Breckland; they have ravaged them almost as savagely as if a state of hostility actually obtained. – *Olive Cook, 1956. (Breckland)*.

Though it has no stupendous mountains furnishing traits of the grand, and no bold and towering cliffs, except a few washed by the ocean, there are many exceptions to the prevailing uniformity of its appearance, particularly in the northern parts, where the general surface is broken into moderate elevations and depressions; where turf-clad hills and fertile valleys are diversified by woods, plantations, hedgerows and other enlivening sylvan decorations, combining all the softer beauties of nature. – *William White, 1845 (White's 1845 Norfolk)*.

Not all Broadland villages have succumbed to tourist pressure. Stokesby, Ranworth and Belaugh are among those which retain a charm derived not only from their location but from the use of local building materials; clay pantiles or reed and sedge for roofs, red clay bricks for walls and flint for churches. – *Derrik Mercer, 1988 (Rural England – Our Countryside At The Crosroads)*.

Norfolk's population is now one of the fastest growing in the United Kingdom. Although this brings much-needed investment to what has been a rural backwater, it is all the more important that an awareness of the past should be the basis of planning for the future. – *Susanna Wade Martins, 1988 (Norfolk – A Changing Countryside)*.

Norfolk companions plodding along to lighten the load together at day's end.